CookingLight®

BREADS, GRAINS & PASTAS

Cooking Light®

BREADS, GRAINS & PASTAS

80 Hearty and Flavorful Recipes for Breads, Biscuits, Waffles, Rice, Macaroni–and Much More

WARNER BOOKS

A Time Warner Company

PHOTOGRAPHER: *Jim Bathie*

PHOTO STYLIST: *Kay E. Clarke*

BOOK DESIGN: *Giorgetta Bell McRee*

COVER DESIGN: *Andrew Newman*

Warner Books, Inc., 666 Fifth Avenue, New York, NY 10103

 A Time Warner Company

Printed in the United States of America
First printing: February 1991
10 9 8 7 6 5 4 3 2 1

Library of Congress Cataloging-in-Publication Data

Cooking light breads, grains, and pastas.
    p.   cm.—(Cooking light)
   Includes index.
   ISBN 0–446–39182–4
   1. Bread. 2. Cookery (Cereals) 3. Cookery (Pasta) I. Title:
Breads, grains, and pastas. II. Series: Cooking light (New York, N.Y.)
TX769.C596 1991
641.8'15—dc20   90–12856
                                                CIP

CONTENTS

EATING WELL IS THE BEST REWARD

Welcome to **Cooking Light**, a cookbook that celebrates the pleasures of good health. These low-fat, low-calorie recipes are easy to make, a delight to behold, and a feast for the senses.

Guided by the belief that good health and good food are synonymous, **Cooking Light** provides an approach to eating and cooking that is both healthy and appealing. Using the eighty recipes in this book, you will see how easy it is to minimize fat and sodium while maximizing minerals, fiber, and vitamins. And you will be delighted by the emphasis on the good taste and texture of fresh wholesome food cooked the light way.

So eat hearty, slim down and delight yourself, your family, and your friends with these easy-to-prepare, all-natural, and very delicious recipes.

EDITOR'S NOTE

Unless otherwise indicated:

eggs are large

margarine is corn oil margarine

sugar is granulated white sugar

flour is all-purpose

two knives can be used instead of a pastry blender

raisins are "dark"

muffin pans are 2½ inches

cranberries and other ingredients are fresh

prepared mustard is regular store-bought yellow mustard

all noodles are cooked without fat or salt

Dutch process cocoa is alkalized

chicken breast is cooked without skin and without salt

vinegar is regular distilled vinegar

Cooking Light®

BREADS, GRAINS & PASTAS

BREADS

Bagels

WHOLE WHEAT–ONION BAGELS

1 package dry yeast
1 cup warm water (105° to 115°)
3 tablespoons instant minced onion
1 tablespoon vegetable oil
1½ cups whole wheat flour
½ teaspoon salt
1¼ cups all-purpose flour
Vegetable cooking spray
3½ quarts water
1 egg
1 tablespoon water
1 tablespoon caraway seeds

Dissolve yeast in the warm water in a large bowl; let stand 5 minutes. Add onion and vegetable oil, stirring well. Stir in whole wheat flour and salt; gradually stir in all-purpose flour. Turn dough out onto a lightly floured surface; knead 1 minute. Cover and let rest 10 minutes. Knead an additional 7 to 10 minutes or until smooth and elastic. Place dough in a large bowl coated with cooking spray, turning to grease top. Cover and let rise in a warm place (85°), free from drafts, 1½ hours or until doubled in bulk.

Punch dough down, and divide into 12 equal portions. Shape each portion into a smooth ball; punch a hole in the center of each ball, using floured fingers. Gently pull dough away from center, making a 1½-inch hole. Place shaped bagels on a baking sheet coated with cooking spray.

Bring 3½ quarts water to a boil in a large Dutch oven. Lower bagels, a few at a time, into gently boiling water; cook 3 minutes on each side. Transfer bagels to a baking sheet coated with cooking spray, using a slotted spoon. Combine egg and 1 tablespoon water; beat well, and gently brush over bagels. Sprinkle with caraway seeds. Bake at 450° for 20 minutes or until golden brown. Cool on wire racks. Yield: 1 dozen (127 calories each).

PROTEIN 4.5 / FAT 2.2 / CARBOHYDRATE 23.2 / FIBER 1.7 / CHOLESTEROL 23 / SODIUM 107 / POTASSIUM 111

Biscuits

ORANGE PINWHEEL BISCUITS

2⅓ cups all-purpose flour
1 tablespoon baking powder
½ teaspoon salt
¼ cup plus 1 tablespoon margarine, softened
½ cup skim milk
⅔ cup plus 3 tablespoons unsweetened orange juice
1 egg, lightly beaten
1 tablespoon margarine, melted
3 tablespoons plus 1 teaspoon sugar, divided
2 teaspoons grated orange rind
½ teaspoon ground allspice
Vegetable cooking spray
1½ teaspoons cornstarch

Combine flour, baking powder, and salt in a large bowl; stir well. Cut in margarine with a pastry blender until mixture resembles coarse meal. Make a well in center of mixture. Combine milk, 3 tablespoons orange juice, and egg. Add to dry ingredients, stirring just until dry ingredients are moistened.

Turn dough out onto a heavily floured surface; knead 10 to 12 times. Chill dough 15 minutes. Roll dough into a 12- x 8-inch rectangle on a lightly floured surface. Brush with melted margarine. Combine 3 tablespoons sugar, orange rind, and allspice; stir well. Sprinkle evenly over dough. Roll up jelly roll fashion, beginning at long side. Pinch edges to seal. Chill roll 30 minutes. Cut roll into sixteen ¾-inch slices; place slices, cut side down, in muffin pans coated with cooking spray. Bake at 400° for 14 minutes.

Combine remaining ⅔ cup orange juice, cornstarch, and remaining 1 teaspoon sugar in a small saucepan. Cook over medium heat, stirring constantly, until thickened. Drizzle 2 teaspoons glaze over each biscuit. Yield: 16 biscuits (136 calories each).

PROTEIN 2.9 / FAT 4.9 / CARBOHYDRATE 20.1 / CHOLESTEROL 17 / IRON 0.7 / SODIUM 189 / CALCIUM 54

ANGEL BISCUITS

---

1 package dry yeast
2 tablespoons warm water (105° to 115°)
1 cup nonfat buttermilk
2½ cups all-purpose flour
1½ teaspoons sugar
1 teaspoon baking powder
½ teaspoon salt
¼ teaspoon baking soda
3 tablespoons shortening
Vegetable cooking spray

Dissolve yeast in 2 tablespoons warm water; let stand 5 minutes. Stir buttermilk into yeast mixture; set aside.

Combine flour and next 4 ingredients in a large bowl; cut in shortening with a pastry blender until mixture resembles coarse meal. Add buttermilk mixture, stirring with a fork until dry ingredients are moistened. Turn dough out onto a lightly floured surface, and knead lightly 3 or 4 times.

Roll dough to ½-inch thickness; cut into rounds with a 2½-inch biscuit cutter. Place biscuits on a baking sheet that has been coated with cooking spray. Cover and let rise in a warm place (85°), free from drafts, for 10 to 15 minutes. Bake at 400° for 10 to 12 minutes or until golden. Yield: 1 dozen (139 calories each).

PROTEIN 3.9 / FAT 3.1 / CARBOHYDRATE 23.5 / CHOLESTEROL 0 / IRON 0.9 / SODIUM 162 / CALCIUM 25

Buns

RAISIN AND RYE BUNS

¾ **cup raisins**
1 **package dry yeast**
1½ **cups warm water (105° to 115°)**
2 **tablespoons firmly packed brown sugar**
2 **tablespoons dark molasses**
2 **tablespoons margarine, melted and cooled**
¼ **teaspoon salt**
2¼ **cups all-purpose flour**
2 **cups rye flour**
Vegetable cooking spray

Place raisins in a bowl of water; let stand 5 minutes. Drain; set aside. Dissolve yeast in 1½ cups warm water in a bowl; let stand 5 minutes. Add brown sugar, molasses, margarine, salt, and flour; beat well. Stir raisins and rye flour into mixture to form a soft dough.

Turn dough out onto a lightly floured surface; knead 8 to 10 minutes or until smooth and elastic. Place dough in a large bowl coated with cooking spray, turning to grease top. Cover and let rise in a warm place (85°), free from drafts, 1½ hours or until doubled in bulk.

Coat two 9-inch cake pans with cooking spray; set aside. Punch dough down; shape dough into 26 (1½-inch) balls, and place in prepared pans. Cover and let rise in a warm place, free from drafts, 45 minutes or until doubled in bulk. Bake at 400° for 20 minutes or until golden brown. Yield: 26 rolls (96 calories each).

PROTEIN 2.1 / FAT 1.1 / CARBOHYDRATE 19.6 / FIBER 0.9 / CHOLESTEROL 0 / SODIUM 36 / POTASSIUM 81

GLAZED ORANGE–RUM BUNS

3½ cups all-purpose flour, divided
1 package dry yeast
½ teaspoon salt
½ cup skim milk
¼ cup plus 2 tablespoons sugar, divided
2 tablespoons unsalted margarine
1 egg
½ cup plus 2 tablespoons unsweetened orange juice,
    divided
2 teaspoons rum extract, divided
Vegetable cooking spray
2 tablespoons unsalted margarine, melted
¼ cup raisins, chopped
1 teaspoon grated orange rind
½ cup low-sugar orange marmalade

Combine 1 cup flour, yeast, and salt in a large bowl; set aside. Combine milk, 2 tablespoons sugar, and margarine in a small saucepan; cook over low heat, stirring constantly, until mixture reaches 120° to 130°. Stir milk mixture into flour mixture. Add egg and ½ cup orange juice. Beat at low speed of an electric mixer until well blended. Beat an additional 3 minutes at medium speed. Add remaining 2½ cups flour and 1½ teaspoons rum extract; stir well.

Turn dough out onto a lightly floured surface, and knead for 8 to

10 minutes or until dough is smooth and elastic. Place dough in a large bowl that has been coated with cooking spray, turning to grease top. Cover and let rise in a warm place (85°), free from drafts, 1 hour or until doubled in bulk.

Punch dough down, and divide in half. Turn dough out onto a lightly floured surface. Roll each half into a 12- x 5-inch rectangle. Brush each rectangle with 1 tablespoon melted margarine. Combine remaining ¼ cup sugar, chopped raisins, and grated orange rind; stir well. Sprinkle half of sugar mixture over each rectangle. Roll up jelly roll fashion, beginning at long side. Pinch ends and seam to seal, and tuck ends under. Cut each rectangle into 12 (1-inch) slices. Place slices, cut side down, in muffin pans that have been coated with cooking spray. Cover and let rise in a warm place, free from drafts, for 1 hour or until doubled in bulk. Bake at 400° for 12 minutes or until golden brown. Remove muffin pans from oven.

Combine orange marmalade, remaining 2 tablespoons orange juice, and ½ teaspoon rum extract in a small saucepan. Cook over low heat, stirring frequently, until marmalade melts. Remove from heat; let cool 2 to 3 minutes. Spoon marmalade mixture evenly over warm buns. Remove from muffin pans, and let cool on wire racks. Yield: 2 dozen (127 calories each).

PROTEIN 2.7 / FAT 2.6 / CARBOHYDRATE 22.6 / CHOLESTEROL 12 / IRON 0.7 / SODIUM 55 / CALCIUM 13

Coffee Cakes

MAPLE OAT BRAN COFFEE CAKE

1 cup unprocessed oat bran
½ cup all-purpose flour
2 tablespoons firmly packed brown sugar, divided
1 tablespoon baking powder
1 teaspoon ground cinnamon
½ teaspoon ground nutmeg
⅓ cup margarine, softened
1 egg plus 1 egg white, beaten
½ cup skim milk
¼ cup reduced-calorie maple syrup
2 teaspoons vanilla extract
Vegetable cooking spray
2 tablespoons wheat germ

Combine oat bran, flour, 1 tablespoon brown sugar, baking powder, cinnamon, and nutmeg; stir well. Cut in margarine with a pastry blender until mixture resembles coarse meal.

Combine egg and egg white, milk, syrup, and vanilla; add to oat bran mixture, stirring just until dry ingredients are moistened.

Spoon mixture into an 8-inch round cake pan heavily coated with cooking spray. Combine wheat germ and remaining brown sugar, sprinkle over top. Bake at 375° for 30 minutes or until a wooden pick inserted in center comes out clean. Cool in pan on a wire rack. Serve warm or at room temperature. Yield: 10 servings (152 calories per serving).

PROTEIN 4.4 / FAT 7.9 / CARBOHYDRATE 15.9 / CHOLESTEROL 28 / IRON 1.0 / SODIUM 183 / CALCIUM 91

CARDAMOM COFFEE BRAID

1 package dry yeast
½ cup warm water (105° to 115°)
1 egg, beaten
3 tablespoons sugar
1 tablespoon margarine
½ teaspoon salt
1 cup skim milk, scalded
½ teaspoon ground cardamom
3 to 3½ cups bread flour
Vegetable cooking spray
1 egg yolk
1 tablespoon water

Dissolve yeast in the warm water in a large bowl; let stand 5 minutes. Stir in egg.

Add sugar, margarine, salt, and cardamom to scalded milk, stirring well. Cool to lukewarm (105° to 115°). Add to yeast mixture, stirring well. Gradually stir in enough flour to make a soft dough.

Turn dough out onto a lightly floured surface; knead 5 minutes or until smooth and elastic. Place dough in a large bowl coated with cooking spray, turning to grease top. Cover and let rise in a warm place (85°), free from drafts, 1½ hours or until doubled in bulk.

Punch dough down; turn out onto a lightly floured surface. Divide dough into 6 equal portions; shape each portion into a 14-inch rope. Braid 3 ropes together, pinching ends to seal. Place braided loaf on a baking sheet coated with cooking spray, tucking ends under. Repeat procedure with remaining ropes to make second loaf.

Cover and let rise in a warm place, free from drafts, 45 minutes or until doubled in bulk. Combine egg yolk and 1 tablespoon water; beat well, and gently brush over loaves. Bake at 350° for 25 minutes or until loaves sound hollow when tapped. Cool on wire racks. Yield: 2 loaves or 24 (1-inch) slices (73 calories per slice).

PROTEIN 2.5 / FAT 1.1 / CARBOHYDRATE 13.0 / FIBER 0.4 / CHOLESTEROL 23 / SODIUM 64 / POTASSIUM 41

Corn Sticks

BUTTERMILK CORN STICKS

1½ cups cornmeal
1½ teaspoons baking powder
¾ teaspoon baking soda
½ teaspoon sugar
½ teaspoon salt
1 egg, lightly beaten
1½ cups buttermilk
Vegetable cooking spray

Combine first 5 ingredients in a large bowl. Combine egg and buttermilk in a small bowl, beating well; add to cornmeal mixture, and stir just until combined.

Place cast-iron corn stick pans coated with cooking spray in a 400° oven for 3 minutes or until very hot. Remove from oven; spoon batter into pans, filling three-fourths full. Bake at 400° for 25 minutes or until golden brown. Yield: 17 corn sticks (48 calories each).

PROTEIN 2.1 / FAT 0.9 / CARBOHYDRATE 7.6 / FIBER 1.6 / CHOLESTEROL 17 / SODIUM 138 / POTASSIUM 68

Crackers

NUTTY WHOLE-GRAIN CRACKERS

1½ cups quick-cooking oats, uncooked
½ cup all-purpose flour
½ cup whole wheat flour
¼ cup wheat germ
¼ cup ground walnuts
1 tablespoon sugar
⅔ cup water
¼ cup vegetable oil
2 teaspoons water, divided
¼ teaspoon salt, divided

Combine first 6 ingredients in a large bowl; stir well. Add ⅔ cup water and vegetable oil, stirring just until dry ingredients are moistened.

Divide dough in half. Roll half of dough into a 12- x 12-inch square on an ungreased baking sheet. Cut into thirty-six 2-inch squares. Brush dough with 1 teaspoon water; sprinkle evenly with ⅛ teaspoon salt. Repeat procedure with remaining half of dough. Bake at 350° for 25 minutes or until crisp and lightly browned.

Separate crackers; remove from baking sheets, and cool on wire racks. Store in an airtight container. Yield: 6 dozen crackers (32 calories each).

PROTEIN 1.0 / FAT 1.3 / CARBOHYDRATE 4.2 / CHOLESTEROL 0 / IRON 0.3 / SODIUM 8 / CALCIUM 3

Crescents

POTATO CRESCENTS

1 cup skim milk
¼ cup unsalted margarine
1 cup cooked, mashed potatoes (cooked without salt or fat)
2 tablespoons brown sugar
1 package dry yeast
½ teaspoon salt
1 egg
3 cups all-purpose flour, divided
1 tablespoon minced fresh chives
Vegetable cooking spray

Combine milk and margarine in a small saucepan; cook over low heat until margarine melts. Let cool to lukewarm (105° to 115°).

Combine milk mixture, potatoes, brown sugar, yeast, salt, egg, and 1 cup flour in a large bowl; beat at low speed of an electric mixer until moistened. Beat at medium speed 3 minutes. Stir in chives and enough remaining flour to make a soft dough.

Turn dough out onto a lightly floured surface, and knead for 8 to 10 minutes or until smooth and elastic. Place in a bowl coated with cooking spray, turning to grease top. Cover and let rise in a warm place (85°), free from drafts, 1 hour or until doubled in bulk.

Punch dough down, and turn out onto a lightly floured surface; roll into a 16-inch circle, and cut into 20 wedges. Roll up each wedge tightly, beginning at wide end. Seal points; place rolls, point side down, on baking sheets coated with cooking spray. Cover and let rise in a warm place (85°), free from drafts, 45 minutes or until doubled in bulk. Bake at 400° for 15 to 18 minutes or until lightly browned. Yield: 20 rolls (103 calories each).

PROTEIN 2.9 / FAT 3.1 / CARBOHYDRATE 16.0 / FIBER 0.2 / CHOLESTEROL 14 / SODIUM 75 / POTASSIUM 85

Danish

APPLE DANISH

½ cup sliced almonds
½ cup skim milk
½ cup unsweetened apple juice, divided
¼ cup plus 2 tablespoons honey, divided
¼ cup unsalted margarine
4½ cups all-purpose flour
½ teaspoon salt
½ teaspoon ground cinnamon
2 eggs
1 package dry yeast
1 cup grated cooking apple
½ teaspoon almond extract
Vegetable cooking spray
Baked Apple Filling
1 egg white, beaten

Place almonds in an electric blender, and process until ground to a powder; set aside. Combine skim milk, ¼ cup apple juice, ¼ cup honey, and margarine in a saucepan, and cook until margarine melts; let cool to 105° to 115°. Combine almond powder, flour, salt, and cinnamon. Combine 2 cups almond-flour mixture with milk mixture, eggs, yeast, apple, and almond extract. Beat at medium speed of an electric mixer 3 minutes; stir in enough almond-flour mixture to make a smooth dough.

Turn dough out onto a lightly floured surface, and knead for 8 to 10 minutes or until smooth and elastic. Place in a bowl coated with cooking spray, turning to grease top. Cover and let rise in a warm place (85°), free from drafts, 1 hour or until doubled in bulk.

Punch dough down; turn out onto a lightly floured surface, and roll into a 24- x 16-inch rectangle. Cut into twenty-four 4-inch squares. Spoon 2 tablespoons Baked Apple Filling onto center of each square, and fold corners toward center, overlapping slightly. Pinch corners and edges together to seal. Place pastries on 2 baking sheets coated with cooking spray; cover and let rise in a warm place (85°), free from drafts, 45 minutes or until doubled in bulk.

Brush pastries with egg white. Bake at 350° for 20 minutes. Combine remaining ¼ cup apple juice and 2 tablespoons honey in a small saucepan; cook until thoroughly heated. Brush hot pastries with glaze. Serve warm. Yield: 2 dozen (154 calories each).

Baked Apple Filling:

6½ cups sliced, peeled cooking apples
Vegetable cooking spray
1 tablespoon plus 1½ teaspoons brown sugar
1 teaspoon ground cinnamon
2½ teaspoons vanilla extract

Arrange apples in a deep baking dish coated with cooking spray. Combine remaining ingredients; sprinkle over apples, and toss. Cover and bake at 350° for 45 to 50 minutes or until softened. Yield: 3 cups (9 calories per tablespoon).

PROTEIN 3.7 / FAT 3.8 / CARBOHYDRATE 27.2 / FIBER 0.9 / CHOLESTEROL 23 / SODIUM 62 / POTASSIUM 110

Loaves

GARDEN BATTER BREAD

2 cups all-purpose flour
1 package dry yeast
½ teaspoon salt
1 cup water
2 tablespoons vegetable oil
1 tablespoon molasses
1 egg
1 cup whole wheat flour
½ cup wheat germ
1 cup finely shredded carrot
1 medium onion, minced
¼ cup minced fresh parsley
½ teaspoon celery seeds
¼ teaspoon pepper
¼ teaspoon dried whole tarragon
1 clove garlic, minced
Vegetable cooking spray

Combine all-purpose flour, yeast, and salt in a large bowl; set aside.

Combine water, vegetable oil, and molasses in a saucepan; cook over medium heat until very warm (120° to 130°). Add molasses mixture and egg to flour mixture; beat at low speed of an electric mixer until blended. Beat an additional 3 minutes at high speed. Add whole wheat flour and wheat germ; mix well. Stir in carrot, onion, parsley, celery seeds, pepper, tarragon, and garlic.

Spoon mixture into a 2-quart soufflé dish that has been coated with cooking spray. Cover and let rise in a warm place (85°), free from drafts, 1 hour and 15 minutes or until doubled in bulk. Bake at 350° for 1 hour or until loaf sounds hollow when tapped. Cool on a wire rack. Yield: 14 servings (149 calories per ½-inch wedge).

PROTEIN 5.3 / FAT 3.3 / CARBOHYDRATE 25.6 / CHOLESTEROL 20 / IRON 1.6 / SODIUM 93 / CALCIUM 23

CRACKED WHEAT–ZUCCHINI BREAD

½ cup boiling water
½ cup uncooked cracked wheat
1 package dry yeast
¼ cup warm water (105° to 115°)
½ cup skim milk
2 tablespoons unsalted margarine
2 tablespoons brown sugar
1 egg, beaten
½ teaspoon salt
½ teaspoon ground cinnamon
¼ teaspoon ground nutmeg
1 cup whole wheat flour
2 cups shredded zucchini
3½ cups all-purpose flour
Vegetable cooking spray

Pour the boiling water over cracked wheat in a small bowl; set aside. Dissolve yeast in the warm water in a large bowl; let stand 5 minutes.

Combine skim milk, margarine, and brown sugar in a small saucepan; cook over medium heat until lukewarm (105° to 115°). Stir in egg, salt, cinnamon, and nutmeg. Add milk mixture to reserved yeast mixture. Add whole wheat flour; beat at low speed of an electric mixer until well blended. Beat an additional 3 minutes at high speed. Stir in reserved cracked wheat mixture, zucchini, and enough flour to make a soft dough.

Turn dough out onto a lightly floured surface, and knead until dough is smooth and elastic (about 8 to 10 minutes). Place dough in a large bowl that has been coated with cooking spray, turning to grease top. Cover and let rise in a warm place (85°), free from drafts, 1 hour or until doubled in bulk.

Punch dough down; cover and let stand 10 minutes. Shape dough into a round loaf. Place in a 9-inch round cake pan that has been coated with cooking spray. Cover and let rise in a warm place, free from drafts, 30 minutes or until doubled in bulk. Bake at 425° for 10 minutes. Reduce heat to 350°, and bake an additional 30 minutes or until loaf sounds hollow when tapped. Remove from pan, and let cool on a wire rack. Yield: 18 servings (141 calories per 1-inch wedge).

PROTEIN 4.6 / FAT 2.0 / CARBOHYDRATE 26.8 / CHOLESTEROL 15 / IRON 1.5 / SODIUM 75 / CALCIUM 19

TOMATO-MOZZARELLA BREAD

1 (16-ounce) loaf unsliced Italian bread
2 tablespoons margarine, melted
1 tablespoon olive oil
2 medium tomatoes, thinly sliced
½ teaspoon dried whole basil
⅔ cup (2⅔ ounces) shredded part-skim mozzarella cheese

Slice bread in half crosswise; reserve one half for other uses. Slice remaining bread in half lengthwise. Place bread slices on a baking sheet, and broil 6 inches from heating element until lightly browned.

Combine margarine and olive oil. Brush over bread slices. Arrange tomato slices evenly over bread. Sprinkle with basil. Top with shredded cheese. Broil 6 inches from heating element until cheese melts. Yield: 8 servings (149 calories per serving).

PROTEIN 5.2 / FAT 6.3 / CARBOHYDRATE 17.8 / CHOLESTEROL 6 / IRON 0.8 / SODIUM 246 / CALCIUM 70

EASY CUCUMBER-DILL LOAF

1½ cups peeled, shredded cucumber
3 cups all-purpose flour, divided
1 package dry yeast
¼ cup warm water (105° to 115°)
1 (8-ounce) carton plain nonfat yogurt
¼ teaspoon baking soda
1 egg
1 tablespoon sugar
½ teaspoon salt
3 tablespoons minced fresh parsley
1 tablespoon minced fresh dillweed or 1 teaspoon dried
  whole dillweed
1 tablespoon minced fresh chives
Vegetable cooking spray

Press cucumber between paper towels to remove excess moisture. Toss cucumber with 2 tablespoons flour; set aside.

Dissolve yeast in the warm water; let stand 5 minutes. Combine yogurt and baking soda in a small bowl; stir well.

Combine egg, sugar, salt, yeast mixture, yogurt mixture, and 2 cups flour in a large bowl. Beat at low speed of an electric mixer until smooth. Beat an additional 3 minutes at high speed. Add remaining ¾ cup plus 2 tablespoons flour; stir well. Stir in reserved cucumber, parsley, dillweed, and chives.

Spoon mixture into a 2-quart soufflé dish that has been coated with cooking spray. Cover and let rise in a warm place (85°), free from drafts, 1 hour or until doubled in bulk. Uncover and bake at 350° for 45 minutes or until loaf sounds hollow when tapped. Remove from dish, and let cool on a wire rack. Yield: 1 loaf or 14 (½-inch) wedges (129 calories per wedge).

PROTEIN 4.8 / FAT 0.8 / CARBOHYDRATE 25.4 / CHOLESTEROL 15 / IRON 1.2 / SODIUM 118 / CALCIUM 48

GRANOLA LOAF

1 cup whole wheat flour
1 package dry yeast
½ teaspoon salt
1 cup skim milk
½ cup water
3 tablespoons honey
2 tablespoons margarine
1 egg
¼ cup all-natural granola cereal
2 tablespoons unsalted sunflower kernels, toasted
2 teaspoons grated orange rind
2 to 2½ cups all-purpose flour
Vegetable cooking spray

Combine whole wheat flour, yeast, and salt in a large bowl; set aside.

Combine skim milk, water, honey, and margarine in a small saucepan; cook over medium heat until very warm (120° to 130°). Add milk mixture and egg to reserved flour mixture; beat at low speed of an electric mixer until well blended. Beat at medium speed an additional 3 minutes. Stir in cereal, sunflower kernels, orange rind, and enough flour to make a soft dough.

Turn dough out onto a lightly floured surface; knead about 8 to 10 minutes or until smooth and elastic. Place dough in a large bowl coated with cooking spray, turning to grease top. Cover and let rise in a warm place (85°), free from drafts, 1 hour or until doubled in bulk.

Punch dough down. Turn dough out onto a lightly floured surface; knead 4 to 5 times. Shape dough into a loaf. Place in a 9- x 5- x 3-inch loaf pan coated with cooking spray. Cover and let rise in a warm place, free from drafts, 40 minutes or until doubled in bulk. Bake at 375° for 30 minutes or until loaf sounds hollow when tapped. Transfer loaf to a wire rack immediately; cool before slicing. Yield: 1 loaf or 18 (½-inch) slices (123 calories per slice).

PROTEIN 3.9 / FAT 2.7 / CARBOHYDRATE 21.4 / FIBER 1.1 / CHOLESTEROL 15 / SODIUM 96 / POTASSIUM 89

ORANGE-PINEAPPLE BREAD

1½ cups whole wheat flour
1 cup all-purpose flour
2 teaspoons baking powder
¼ teaspoon baking soda
¼ teaspoon salt
¼ cup firmly packed brown sugar
¼ cup vegetable oil
1 egg, beaten
2 teaspoons grated orange rind
½ cup unsweetened orange juice
1 (8-ounce) can unsweetened crushed pineapple,
    undrained
Vegetable cooking spray

Combine first 5 ingredients, and set aside.

Combine brown sugar, oil, and egg; mix well. Stir in orange rind, juice, and pineapple. Stir in dry ingredients, blending until smooth.

Spoon batter into an 8½- x 4½- x 3-inch loaf pan coated with cooking spray. Bake at 350° for 1 hour or until a wooden pick inserted in center comes out clean. Yield: 1 loaf or 17 (½-inch) slices (121 calories per slice).

PROTEIN 2.7 / FAT 3.8 / CARBOHYDRATE 19.8 / FIBER 1.1 / CHOLESTEROL 16 / SODIUM 81 / POTASSIUM 96

SAUSAGE AND PEPPER BRAID

1 cup skim milk
2 tablespoons unsalted margarine
2 tablespoons honey
1 package dry yeast
1 tablespoon dried whole sage
¼ teaspoon salt

1 egg
3½ to 4 cups all-purpose flour, divided
Vegetable cooking spray
1 pound sweet Italian sausage, cooked and well drained
1 cup finely chopped green pepper
1 cup finely chopped red pepper

Combine skim milk, margarine, and honey in a small saucepan. Cook over low heat until margarine melts; let cool to lukewarm (105° to 115°). Combine milk mixture, yeast, sage, salt, egg, and 1 cup flour in a large bowl; beat at low speed of an electric mixer until moistened. Beat at medium speed 3 minutes. Stir in enough remaining flour to make a soft dough.

Turn dough out onto a lightly floured surface and knead for 8 to 10 minutes or until smooth and elastic. Place in a large bowl coated with cooking spray, turning to grease top. Cover and let rise in a warm place (85°), free from drafts, 1 hour or until doubled in bulk.

Punch dough down, and divide into 3 equal portions. Roll 1 portion into an 18- x 10-inch rectangle. Sprinkle with sausage, and roll up jelly roll fashion, starting with long side. Pinch edges of seam together; set aside. Repeat procedure with second portion of dough, sprinkling dough with green pepper; set aside. Repeat procedure with remaining dough, sprinkling with red pepper.

Place dough rolls on a baking sheet coated with cooking spray. Braid dough rolls together, gently stretching to 22 inches in length. Fold ends under.

Cover and let rise in a warm place (85°), free from drafts, 45 minutes or until doubled in bulk. Bake at 400° for 20 minutes or until golden brown. Cool 10 minutes. Slice with an electric knife; serve warm. Yield: 1 (20-inch) loaf or 26 (¾-inch) slices (119 calories per slice).

PROTEIN 5.0 / FAT 4.6 / CARBOHYDRATE 14.4 / FIBER 0.1 / CHOLESTEROL 21 / SODIUM 150 / POTASSIUM 106

EGGPLANT BREAD

1½ cups finely chopped, peeled eggplant
½ cup finely chopped onion
¾ cup dry red wine
¾ teaspoon dried whole oregano
¾ teaspoon dried whole basil
1 cup plus 2 tablespoons skim milk
2 tablespoons unsalted margarine
1 tablespoon plus 1½ teaspoons honey
1 package dry yeast
¼ teaspoon salt
1 egg white
3½ cups all-purpose flour, divided
Vegetable cooking spray
¾ cup (3 ounces) finely shredded part-skim mozzarella
  cheese

Combine first 5 ingredients in a saucepan, and bring to a boil. Cover; reduce heat, and simmer 5 minutes. Drain well; set aside.

Combine skim milk, margarine, and honey in a small saucepan. Cook over low heat until margarine melts, and let cool to lukewarm (105° to 115°). Combine milk mixture, yeast, salt, egg white, and 1 cup flour in a large bowl. Beat at low speed of an electric mixer just until dry ingredients are moistened. Beat at medium speed 3 minutes. Stir in enough remaining flour to make a soft dough.

Turn dough out onto a lightly floured surface, and knead for 8 to 10 minutes or until smooth and elastic. Place in a bowl coated with cooking spray, turning to grease top. Cover and let rise in a warm place (85°), free from drafts, 1 hour or until doubled in bulk.

Punch dough down, and divide in half. Roll each half into an 18- x 10-inch rectangle. Spread half of eggplant mixture on each rectangle, leaving a ½-inch border on all sides; sprinkle with cheese. Roll up dough jelly roll fashion, beginning with long side. Pinch edges of seam together, and seal ends.

Place 2 rolls side by side on a baking sheet coated with cooking spray; twist rolls together several times. Shape twisted roll into a ring, pinching ends together. Cover and let rise in a warm place (85°), free from drafts, 45 minutes to 1 hour or until doubled in bulk. Bake at 400° for 30 to 35 minutes or until golden brown. Slice with an electric knife. Yield: 1 ring or 50 (½-inch) slices (46 calories per slice).

PROTEIN 1.7 / FAT 0.8 / CARBOHYDRATE 7.5 / FIBER 0.1 / CHOLESTEROL 1 / SODIUM 25 / POTASSIUM 46

GREEN ONION RYE BREAD

½ cup water
1 teaspoon chicken-flavored bouillon granules
2 cups minced green onion
1 cup skim milk
¼ cup unsalted margarine
¼ cup light molasses
2 cups all-purpose flour
2 tablespoons brown sugar
2 packages dry yeast
1 teaspoon dried whole rosemary
½ teaspoon salt
4½ cups rye flour
Vegetable cooking spray

Combine water, bouillon granules, and green onion in a saucepan. Cover and cook 5 minutes or until onion is tender; set aside to cool.

Combine skim milk, margarine, and molasses in a small saucepan; cook over low heat, stirring occasionally, until margarine melts. Set aside, and let cool to lukewarm (105° to 115°).

Combine milk mixture, reserved green onion mixture, flour, sugar, yeast, rosemary, and salt in a large bowl. Beat at low speed of an electric mixer until moistened. Beat at medium speed 3 minutes. Stir in enough rye flour to make a stiff dough.

Turn dough out onto a lightly floured surface, and knead for 8 to 10 minutes until smooth and elastic. Place in a large bowl coated with cooking spray, turning to grease top. Cover and let rise in a warm place (85°), free from drafts, 45 minutes or until doubled in bulk.

Punch dough down. Turn dough out onto a lightly floured surface, and divide in half. Shape each half into a round loaf, and place on a baking sheet coated with cooking spray. Cover and let rise in a warm place (85°), free from drafts, 45 minutes or until doubled in bulk. Cut 3 slashes, evenly spaced, ¼-inch deep, in top of loaf.

Bake at 350° for 40 to 45 minutes or until browned. Cut each loaf into 16 wedges. Yield: 2 loaves or 32 wedges (97 calories per wedge).

PROTEIN 2.4 / FAT 1.6 / CARBOHYDRATE 18.3 / FIBER 0.6 / CHOLESTEROL 0 / SODIUM 54 / POTASSIUM 90

HONEY-GRAIN BREAD

2 packages dry yeast
½ cup warm water (105° to 115°)
½ cup plus 2 tablespoons honey, divided
1 cup skim milk
¼ cup unsalted margarine
1 egg, beaten
½ cup bulgur wheat, uncooked
½ cup wheat germ
1 teaspoon salt
½ teaspoon ground nutmeg
1½ cups whole wheat flour
3¾ to 4½ cups all-purpose flour, divided
Vegetable cooking spray

Dissolve yeast in the warm water in a large bowl; add 2 tablespoons honey, and let stand 5 minutes or until foamy. Combine remaining ½ cup honey, skim milk, and margarine in a saucepan. Cook over low heat until margarine melts; let cool to lukewarm (105° to 115°). Add milk mixture, egg, bulgur, wheat germ, salt, nutmeg, whole wheat flour, and 2 cups all-purpose flour to yeast mixture. Stir in enough remaining all-purpose flour to make a stiff dough.

Turn dough out onto a lightly floured surface, and knead for 8 to 10 minutes or until smooth and elastic. Place in a large bowl coated with cooking spray, turning to grease top. Cover and let rise in a warm place (85°), free from drafts, 1 hour or until doubled in bulk.

Punch dough down, and divide in half; shape each half into a loaf. Place loaves in two 8½- x 4½- x 3-inch loaf pans coated with cooking spray. Repeat rising procedure 45 minutes or until doubled in bulk. Bake at 350° for 30 to 35 minutes or until browned. Yield: 2 loaves or 34 (½-inch) slices (118 calories per slice).

PROTEIN 3.6 / FAT 2.0 / CARBOHYDRATE 22.8 / FIBER 0.6 / CHOLESTEROL 8 / SODIUM 76 / POTASSIUM 80

SWEET POTATO BREAD

2 cups all-purpose flour
2½ teaspoons baking powder
½ teaspoon salt
¼ teaspoon ground allspice
¼ teaspoon ground nutmeg
1 cup cooked, mashed sweet potatoes
½ cup firmly packed brown sugar
¼ cup unsalted margarine, melted
3 tablespoons skim milk
2 eggs
1 teaspoon grated orange rind
¼ cup chopped pecans
Vegetable cooking spray

Combine first 5 ingredients in a large bowl; set aside. Combine potatoes, sugar, margarine, skim milk, eggs, orange rind, and pecans, beating well. Add to dry ingredients, stirring just until moistened. Pour batter into a 9- x 5- x 3-inch loaf pan coated with cooking spray. Bake at 350° for 45 minutes or until a wooden pick inserted in center comes out clean. Cool in pan 10 minutes; remove from pan, and cool completely. Yield: 1 loaf or 18 (½-inch) slices (122 calories per slice).

PROTEIN 2.5 / FAT 4.4 / CARBOHYDRATE 18.6 / FIBER 0.2 / CHOLESTEROL 30 / SODIUM 120 / POTASSIUM 82

CRANBERRY-ORANGE BREAD

1¾ cups all-purpose flour
1 teaspoon baking powder
1 teaspoon baking soda
¼ teaspoon salt
¼ cup plus 2 tablespoons unsalted margarine, softened
¼ cup plus 2 tablespoons sugar
2 eggs, lightly beaten
1 tablespoon grated orange rind
1 cup unsweetened orange juice
1 cup cranberries, chopped
¼ cup chopped walnuts
Vegetable cooking spray

Combine flour, baking powder, baking soda, and salt in a medium bowl; set aside. Cream margarine in a large bowl; gradually add sugar, beating until light and fluffy. Add eggs and orange rind, beating well. Add flour mixture alternately with orange juice, beginning and ending with flour mixture. Mix just until blended after each addition. Stir in chopped cranberries and walnuts. Pour batter into a 9- x 5- x 3-inch loaf pan coated with cooking spray. Bake at 350° for 50 to 55 minutes or until a wooden pick inserted in center comes out clean. Cool in pan 10 minutes; remove from pan, and cool completely before slicing. Yield: 1 loaf or 18 (½-inch) slices (117 calories per slice).

PROTEIN 2.4 / FAT 5.5 / CARBOHYDRATE 15.1 / FIBER 0.2 / CHOLESTEROL 30 / SODIUM 77 / POTASSIUM 61

WHOLE WHEAT–APRICOT TWIST

1 package dry yeast
¼ cup warm water (105° to 115°)
¾ cup nonfat buttermilk
3 tablespoons molasses
2 tablespoons margarine
½ cup bran flakes cereal
1½ cups whole wheat flour
½ teaspoon salt
2 cups chopped, dried apricots
1¼ cups plus 1 tablespoon all-purpose flour, divided
Vegetable cooking spray

Dissolve yeast in the warm water; let stand 5 minutes. Combine buttermilk, molasses, and margarine in a saucepan; cook over medium heat until margarine melts, stirring constantly. Transfer buttermilk mixture to a large bowl; add bran cereal, and stir well. Cool to lukewarm (105° to 115°). Add yeast mixture, whole wheat flour, and salt. Beat at low speed of an electric mixer until well blended. Beat an additional 3 minutes at high speed. Stir in apricots and enough of the 1¼ cups all-purpose flour to make a soft dough.

Sprinkle 1 tablespoon all-purpose flour evenly over work surface. Turn dough out onto floured surface, and knead for 8 to 10 minutes or until smooth and elastic. Place dough in a large bowl that has been coated with cooking spray, turning to grease top. Cover and let rise in a warm place (85°), free from drafts, 1½ hours or until doubled in bulk.

Punch dough down, and divide into 3 equal portions. Shape each portion into an 11-inch rope. Braid ropes, pinching ends to seal. Place braided loaf in a 9- x 5- x 3-inch loaf pan that has been coated with cooking spray. Cover and let rise in a warm place, free from drafts, 45 minutes or until doubled in bulk. Bake at 350° for 30 to 40 minutes or until loaf sounds hollow when tapped. Remove from pan, and let cool completely on a wire rack. Yield: 1 loaf or 18 (½-inch) slices (105 calories per slice).

PROTEIN 3.2 / FAT 1.7 / CARBOHYDRATE 20.2 / CHOLESTEROL 0 / IRON 1.3 / SODIUM 103 / CALCIUM 19

Madeleines

WHOLE WHEAT MADELEINES

1½ cups whole wheat flour
½ cup all-purpose flour
1 tablespoon sugar
1 teaspoon baking powder
¼ teaspoon salt
1¼ cups plus 2 tablespoons skim milk
¼ cup vegetable oil
Vegetable cooking spray

Combine first 5 ingredients in a large bowl; make a well in center of mixture. Combine skim milk and vegetable oil, stirring well. Add to flour mixture, stirring just until dry ingredients are moistened. Spoon batter into 3-inch madeleine pans coated with cooking spray, filling two-thirds full. Bake at 425° for 15 minutes or until lightly browned. Yield: 2½ dozen (50 calories each).

PROTEIN 1.4 / FAT 2.0 / CARBOHYDRATE 7.0 / CHOLESTEROL 0 / IRON 0.3 / SODIUM 36 / CALCIUM 23

Muffins

CRANBERRY-PINEAPPLE MUFFINS

1 cup whole wheat flour
½ cup all-purpose flour
½ cup regular oats, uncooked
¼ cup plus 1 tablespoon sugar, divided
2 teaspoons baking powder
¼ teaspoon salt
¼ cup unsalted margarine
1 egg, beaten
1 cup skim milk
1 cup fresh cranberries, coarsely chopped
½ cup unsweetened crushed pineapple, drained
Vegetable cooking spray
¼ teaspoon ground cinnamon

Combine first 6 ingredients; stir well. Cut in margarine with a pastry blender until mixture resembles coarse meal. Make a well in center of mixture. Combine beaten egg and skim milk; add to dry ingredients, stirring just until moistened. Gently fold in cranberries and pineapple.

Spoon batter into muffin pans that have been coated with cooking spray, filling three-fourths full. Combine remaining 1 tablespoon sugar and cinnamon; sprinkle evenly over muffin batter. Bake at 400° for 20 to 25 minutes or until golden brown. Remove from pans immediately. Yield: 1 dozen (147 calories each).

PROTEIN 3.8 / FAT 5.0 / CARBOHYDRATE 22.8 / CHOLESTEROL 23 / IRON 0.8 / SODIUM 116 / CALCIUM 70

BLUEBERRY ENGLISH MUFFINS

1 package dry yeast
1 cup warm water (105° to 115°)
3¼ cups all-purpose flour, divided
2 tablespoons honey
2 tablespoons unsalted margarine, melted
½ teaspoon salt
1 cup fresh or frozen blueberries, thawed and drained
2 tablespoons cornmeal, divided

Dissolve yeast in the warm water in a large bowl; let stand 5 minutes. Add 2 cups flour, honey, margarine, and salt; mix well. Stir in enough of the remaining 1¼ cups flour to make a soft dough. Gently knead in blueberries.

Turn dough out onto a lightly floured surface; roll to ½-inch thickness. Cut dough into rounds with a 3-inch cutter. Sprinkle 2 baking sheets with 1½ teaspoons cornmeal each. Transfer dough rounds to baking sheets, placing 2 inches apart. Sprinkle remaining 1 tablespoon cornmeal evenly over tops of muffins. Cover and let rise in a warm place (85°) free from drafts, 1 hour or until doubled in bulk.

Heat an electric skillet to medium heat (350°). Using a wide spatula, transfer muffins to skillet, 7 at a time. Cook, partially covered, 5 minutes. Turn muffins over. Cook, partially covered, an additional 8 to 10 minutes. Remove from skillet, and let cool on wire racks. Repeat procedure with remaining muffins. Yield: 14 muffins (150 calories each).

PROTEIN 3.7 / FAT 2.0 / CARBOHYDRATE 29.0 / CHOLESTEROL 0 / IRON 1.1 / SODIUM 85 / CALCIUM 7

PEAR-ALMOND MUFFINS

¼ cup plus 1 tablespoon slivered almonds
1½ cups all-purpose flour
1 tablespoon baking powder
¼ teaspoon salt
½ teaspoon ground cinnamon
⅛ teaspoon ground mace
2 eggs
½ cup buttermilk
¼ cup honey
¼ cup unsweetened pear juice
¼ cup unsalted margarine, melted
½ teaspoon almond extract
1 cup grated pear
Vegetable cooking spray
¼ cup sliced almonds

Place slivered almonds in container of an electric blender, and process to a powder. Combine almond powder, flour, baking powder, salt, cinnamon, and mace in a large bowl; make a well in center of mixture. Combine eggs, buttermilk, honey, pear juice, margarine, and almond extract in a bowl; beat at medium speed of an electric mixer until smooth. Add to flour mixture, stirring just until moistened. Fold in pear. Spoon batter into muffin pans coated with cooking spray, filling two-thirds full. Sprinkle sliced almonds over batter. Bake at 400° for 20 to 25 minutes or until golden brown. Yield: 15 muffins (139 calories each).

PROTEIN 3.3 / FAT 6.3 / CARBOHYDRATE 18.6 / FIBER 0.8 / CHOLESTEROL 37 / SODIUM 118 / POTASSIUM 98

PEANUT BUTTER–BANANA MUFFINS

1½ cups all-purpose flour
¼ cup firmly packed brown sugar
1 tablespoon baking powder
½ teaspoon salt
¾ cup skim milk
½ cup smooth peanut butter
⅓ cup unsalted margarine, melted
2 medium bananas, mashed
1 egg
Vegetable cooking spray

Combine first 4 ingredients in a large bowl; make a well in center of mixture. Combine skim milk, peanut butter, margarine, banana, and egg in a mixing bowl; beat at medium speed of an electric mixer until smooth. Add to flour mixture, stirring just until moistened. Spoon into muffin pans coated with cooking spray, filling two-thirds full. Bake at 400° for 20 to 25 minutes or until golden brown. Yield: 16 muffins (150 calories each).

PROTEIN 4.4 / FAT 8.4 / CARBOHYDRATE 15.8 / FIBER 0.5 / CHOLESTEROL 17 / SODIUM 181 / POTASSIUM 159

CRANBERRY-OATMEAL MUFFINS

1 cup whole wheat flour
¾ cup all-purpose flour
¾ cup regular oats, uncooked
⅓ cup firmly packed brown sugar
2 teaspoons baking powder
½ teaspoon ground cinnamon
⅛ teaspoon salt
1 teaspoon grated orange rind
¼ cup margarine
1 egg, beaten

1 cup skim milk
¾ cup fresh or frozen cranberries, coarsely chopped
Vegetable cooking spray

Combine first 8 ingredients in a large bowl; stir until well blended. Cut in margarine with a pastry blender until mixture resembles coarse meal. Make a well in center of mixture. Combine egg and skim milk in a small bowl; stir until well blended. Add to dry ingredients, stirring just until moistened; gently fold in cranberries.

Spoon batter into muffin pans coated with cooking spray, filling two-thirds full. Bake at 400° for 20 minutes or until lightly browned. Remove from muffin pans, and serve hot. Yield: 14 muffins (136 calories each).

PROTEIN 3.6 / FAT 4.3 / CARBOHYDRATE 21.5 / FIBER 1.6 / CHOLESTEROL 20 / SODIUM 120 / POTASSIUM 112

CARROT MUFFINS

1¼ cups all-purpose flour
½ cup whole wheat flour
1½ teaspoons baking powder
½ teaspoon ground cinnamon
¼ teaspoon ground nutmeg
¼ teaspoon salt
1 cup shredded carrot
¼ cup chopped walnuts
1 cup nonfat buttermilk
2 eggs, beaten
⅓ cup reduced-calorie maple syrup
¼ cup unsalted margarine, melted
Vegetable cooking spray

Combine first 6 ingredients in a large bowl; stir in carrot and walnuts. Make a well in center of mixture. Combine buttermilk, eggs, syrup, and margarine in a bowl; add to dry ingredients, stirring just until moistened. Spoon batter into muffin pans coated with cooking spray, filling two-thirds full. Bake at 400° for 20 minutes or until lightly browned. Serve warm. Yield: 1 dozen (141 calories each).

PROTEIN 4.5 / FAT 6.9 / CARBOHYDRATE 16.0 / FIBER 1.4 / CHOLESTEROL 33 / SODIUM 113 / POTASSIUM 83

OAT BRAN MUFFINS

2½ cups unprocessed oat bran
½ cup raisins
1 tablespoon firmly packed brown sugar
1 tablespoon baking powder
⅛ teaspoon salt
½ cup chunky unsweetened applesauce
1 cup skim milk
½ cup egg substitute or 2 eggs, lightly beaten
1 tablespoon corn oil
Vegetable cooking spray

Combine oat bran, raisins, brown sugar, baking powder, and salt in a large bowl; make a well in center of mixture. Combine applesauce, milk, egg substitute or eggs, and corn oil, stirring well. Add applesauce mixture to dry ingredients, stirring just until moistened.

Coat muffin pans with cooking spray or line with paper baking cups. Spoon batter into pans, filling three-fourths full. Bake at 425° for 20 to 25 minutes or until golden brown. Yield: 1 dozen (124 calories each).

PROTEIN 5.6 / FAT 3.1 / CARBOHYDRATE 18.7 / FIBER 5.3 / CHOLESTEROL 0 / SODIUM 128 / POTASSIUM 207

Pancakes

WHOLE WHEAT–APPLE PANCAKES

1 cup all-purpose flour
1 cup whole wheat flour
2 tablespoons brown sugar
1 tablespoon baking powder
½ teaspoon baking soda
½ teaspoon salt
½ teaspoon ground cinnamon
1½ cups buttermilk
¾ cup unsweetened apple juice
3 tablespoons unsalted margarine, melted
2 eggs
1 cup grated cooking apple
Vegetable cooking spray

Combine first 7 ingredients in a large bowl. Combine buttermilk, apple juice, margarine, and eggs in a bowl, and mix well. Add to flour mixture, stirring until smooth. Stir in apple. Heat a griddle or skillet coated with cooking spray over medium heat until hot. For each pancake, pour 2 tablespoons batter onto griddle. Turn pancakes when tops are bubbly and edges are slightly dry. Yield: 23 (4-inch) pancakes (71 calories each).

PROTEIN 2.3 / FAT 2.3 / CARBOHYDRATE 10.7 / FIBER 0.5 / CHOLESTEROL 24 / SODIUM 121 / POTASSIUM 73

Popovers

WHOLE WHEAT POPOVERS

2 eggs
1 cup skim milk
½ cup all-purpose flour
½ cup whole wheat flour
1 tablespoon unsalted margarine, melted
¼ teaspoon salt
Vegetable cooking spray

Place eggs and skim milk in container of an electric blender; process until bubbly. Add flours, margarine, and salt; process until smooth.

Place a muffin pan coated with cooking spray in a 450° oven for 3 minutes or until very hot. Spoon batter into muffin pan, filling two-thirds full. Bake at 425° for 20 minutes; reduce heat to 350°, and bake for 10 minutes. Prick each popover with a fork to let steam escape, and bake for an additional 5 minutes. Yield: 9 popovers (88 calories each).

PROTEIN 4.0 / FAT 2.7 / CARBOHYDRATE 12.0 / FIBER 0.7 / CHOLESTEROL 61 / SODIUM 95 / POTASSIUM 92

Rolls

POPPY SEED–ONION TWISTS

Vegetable cooking spray
¼ cup minced onion
1 package dry yeast
¼ cup warm water (105° to 115°)
3 tablespoons sugar
3 tablespoons unsalted margarine
1 teaspoon cracked pepper
½ teaspoon salt
¾ cup skim milk
1 egg yolk
1 cup whole wheat flour
2¾ cups all-purpose flour, divided
¼ cup poppy seeds

Coat a small nonstick skillet with cooking spray; place over medium-high heat until hot. Add onion, and sauté until tender. Remove from heat and set aside.

Dissolve yeast in the warm water, and let stand 5 minutes.

Combine sugar, margarine, cracked pepper, salt, and skim milk in a small saucepan. Place over medium heat and cook until margarine melts, stirring occasionally. Place milk mixture in a large bowl; cool to lukewarm (105° to 115°). Add yeast mixture, reserved onion mixture, and egg yolk to milk mixture, stirring well. Gradually add whole wheat flour; stir well. Add 2 cups all-purpose flour to make a soft dough.

Turn dough out onto a lightly floured surface; knead remaining ¾ cup all-purpose flour into dough for 8 to 10 minutes or until smooth and elastic. Place in a large bowl that has been coated with cooking spray, turning to grease top. Cover; let rise in a warm place (85°), free from drafts, 1 hour or until doubled in bulk.

Punch dough down, and divide in half. Roll each half into a 15- x

18-inch rectangle on a lightly floured surface. Lightly spray surface of each rectangle with cooking spray; sprinkle 1 tablespoon poppy seeds over each rectangle. Fold dough in thirds starting with short ends; roll into 15- x 18-inch rectangles. Lightly spray surface of each rectangle with cooking spray; sprinkle 1 tablespoon poppy seeds over each rectangle. Fold dough in thirds starting with short ends; roll into 8-inch squares. Cut dough into 4- x ½-inch strips. Twist strips loosely; place on baking sheets that have been coated with cooking spray. Bake at 400° for 12 minutes or until golden brown. Remove from baking sheets; cool on wire racks. Yield: approximately 5½ dozen (32 calories each).

PROTEIN 0.9 / FAT 1.0 / CARBOHYDRATE 5.0 / CHOLESTEROL 4 / IRON 0.3 / SODIUM 20 / CALCIUM 13

MUSHROOM–SWISS CHEESE ROLLS

1 cup skim milk
¼ cup unsalted margarine
¼ cup honey
½ teaspoon salt
1 teaspoon dried whole thyme
1 package dry yeast
1 egg
3½ cups all-purpose flour, divided
2 cups sliced fresh mushrooms
1 cup (4 ounces) finely shredded Swiss cheese
Vegetable cooking spray

Combine skim milk, margarine, and honey in a small saucepan. Cook over low heat until margarine melts; let cool to lukewarm (105° to 115°).

Combine milk mixture in a large bowl with salt, thyme, yeast, egg, and 1 cup flour; beat at low speed of an electric mixer until moistened. Beat at medium speed 3 minutes. Stir in mushrooms and enough remaining flour to make a soft dough.

Turn dough out onto a lightly floured surface, and knead in cheese. Knead 4 to 6 minutes or until smooth and elastic. Place in a bowl coated with cooking spray, turning to grease top. Cover and let rise in a warm place (85°), free from drafts, 1 hour or until doubled in bulk.

Punch dough down, and divide into 4 portions. Shape each portion into 12 rolls, and place in two 13- x 9- x 2-inch baking pans coated with cooking spray. Cover and let rise in a warm place (85°), free from drafts, 45 minutes or until doubled in bulk. Bake at 350° for 25 to 30 minutes or until golden brown. Yield: 4 dozen (56 calories each).

PROTEIN 2.0 / FAT 1.8 / CARBOHYDRATE 8.3 / FIBER 0.0 / CHOLESTEROL 8 / SODIUM 35 / POTASSIUM 38

HOT CROSS ROLLS

1 package dry yeast
2 tablespoons sugar
¼ cup warm water (105° to 115°)
4¾ cups all-purpose flour, divided
1 teaspoon ground cinnamon
¼ teaspoon salt
¼ teaspoon ground nutmeg
1 cup warm skim milk (105° to 115°)
2 eggs, beaten
¼ cup vegetable oil
⅓ cup currants
Vegetable cooking spray
½ cup sifted powdered sugar
2 teaspoons skim milk

Dissolve yeast and 2 tablespoons sugar in the warm water in a large bowl; let stand 5 minutes or until foamy.

Combine 2 cups flour, cinnamon, salt, and nutmeg in a medium bowl; stir well. Add flour mixture to yeast mixture with warm skim milk; beat at medium speed of electric mixer until smooth. Stir in eggs, oil, and currants. Gradually add enough remaining flour to make a soft dough, stirring well after each addition.

Turn dough out onto a floured surface, and knead 8 to 10 minutes or until smooth and elastic. Place in a bowl coated with cooking spray, turning to grease top. Cover and let rise in a warm place (85°), free from drafts, 1 hour or until doubled in bulk.

Punch dough down, and divide into 24 pieces; shape each piece into a ball. Place balls in muffin pans coated with cooking spray. Cover and let rise in a warm place (85°), free from drafts, 45 minutes or until doubled in bulk. Bake at 375° for 15 minutes. Cool rolls in pans 10 minutes; remove from pans and transfer to cooling racks.

Combine powdered sugar and skim milk, stirring well. Drizzle 1 teaspoon sugar glaze in an X pattern over top of each roll. Yield: 2 dozen rolls (150 calories each).

PROTEIN 3.9 / FAT 3.1 / CARBOHYDRATE 26.3 / CHOLESTEROL 23 / IRON 1.0 / SODIUM 37 / CALCIUM 23

ORANGE RYE ROLLS

2 cups rye flour
1 package dry yeast
½ teaspoon salt
1 cup light beer
1 cup plus 1 tablespoon water, divided
2 tablespoons unsalted margarine
3 tablespoons molasses, divided
1 tablespoon grated orange rind
2 tablespoons fennel seeds
3½ cups plus 2 tablespoons all-purpose flour, divided
Vegetable cooking spray

Combine first 3 ingredients in a large bowl; stir well. Set aside.

Combine beer, 1 cup water, margarine, and 2 tablespoons molasses in a saucepan; cook over medium heat until very warm (120° to 130°). Add beer mixture to flour mixture; beat at medium speed of an electric mixer 2 minutes or until smooth. Stir in orange rind, fennel, and 3½ cups all-purpose flour to make a soft dough.

Sprinkle remaining 2 tablespoons flour over work surface. Turn dough out onto floured surface; knead for 8 to 10 minutes or until smooth and elastic. Place in a large bowl that has been coated with cooking spray, turning to grease top. Cover; let rise in a warm place (85°), free from drafts, 1½ hours or until doubled in bulk.

Punch dough down; divide into 32 portions. Shape each portion into a ball. Place in two 9-inch square baking pans that have been coated with cooking spray. Cover and let rise in a warm place, free from drafts, 45 minutes or until doubled in bulk.

Bake at 350° for 15 minutes. Combine remaining 1 tablespoon molasses and 1 tablespoon water; stir well. Brush rolls gently with molasses mixture. Bake an additional 10 to 15 minutes or until golden. Remove from pans, and cool on wire racks. Yield: 32 rolls (90 calories each).

PROTEIN 2.3 / FAT 1.0 / CARBOHYDRATE 17.7 / CHOLESTEROL 0 / IRON 0.7 / SODIUM 38 / CALCIUM 12

CHEDDAR CHEESE CRESCENT ROLLS

1 package dry yeast
½ cup warm water (105° to 115°)
2 tablespoons unsalted margarine
2 tablespoons sugar
¾ teaspoon ground red pepper
½ teaspoon salt
½ teaspoon garlic powder
½ cup skim milk
¾ cup (3 ounces) finely shredded extra-sharp Cheddar
   cheese
1 egg, beaten
3 cups all-purpose flour, divided
Vegetable cooking spray

Dissolve yeast in the warm water, and let stand 5 minutes.

Combine margarine, sugar, red pepper, salt, garlic powder, and skim milk in a small saucepan; heat until margarine melts, stirring constantly. Transfer milk mixture to a large bowl; cool to lukewarm (105° to 115°). Add yeast mixture, cheese, egg, and 2 cups flour, stirring well. Add enough remaining flour to make a soft dough.

Turn dough out onto a lightly floured surface; knead until dough is smooth and elastic (about 8 to 10 minutes). Place dough in a large bowl that has been coated with cooking spray, turning to grease top. Cover and let rise in a warm place (85°), free from drafts, 1 hour or until doubled in bulk.

Punch dough down; turn onto a lightly floured surface. Cover and let stand 10 minutes. Divide dough in half. Roll each half into a 12-inch circle. Cut each circle into 12 wedges. Roll up each wedge, beginning at wide end. Place wedges, point side down, on baking sheets that have been coated with cooking spray. Cover and let rise in a warm place, free from drafts, 30 minutes or until doubled in bulk. Bake at 425° for 6 minutes or until lightly browned. Yield: 2 dozen (97 calories each).

PROTEIN 3.2 / FAT 2.7 / CARBOHYDRATE 14.6 / CHOLESTEROL 15 / IRON 0.6 / SODIUM 77 / CALCIUM 37

Waffles

GINGERED APPLESAUCE WAFFLES

1 cup whole wheat flour
2 teaspoons sugar
½ teaspoon baking powder
½ teaspoon baking soda
¾ teaspoon ground ginger
1½ cups low-fat buttermilk
½ cup unsweetened applesauce
2 tablespoons vegetable oil
1 egg, separated
Vegetable cooking spray

Combine flour, sugar, baking powder, baking soda, and ginger in a medium bowl, stirring well; set aside.

Combine buttermilk, applesauce, vegetable oil, and egg yolk in a small bowl; mix well, and gradually add to dry ingredients, stirring until smooth.

Beat egg white (at room temperature) in a small bowl until stiff peaks form; gently fold into batter.

Coat a waffle iron with cooking spray; allow waffle iron to preheat. Pour 1¼ cups batter onto hot waffle iron, spreading batter to edges. Bake 3 minutes or until steaming stops. Repeat procedure until all batter is used. Yield: 16 (4-inch) waffles (60 calories each).

PROTEIN 2.2 / FAT 2.4 / CARBOHYDRATE 7.9 / FIBER 0.6 / CHOLESTEROL 18 / SODIUM 49 / POTASSIUM 74

OATMEAL–WHOLE WHEAT WAFFLES

1½ cups plus 2 tablespoons whole wheat flour
2¼ teaspoons baking powder
¼ teaspoon salt
2 cups skim milk
2 eggs, beaten
2 tablespoons unsalted margarine, melted
2 tablespoons honey
1 cup regular oats, uncooked
Vegetable cooking spray

Combine first 3 ingredients in a medium mixing bowl. Add skim milk, eggs, margarine, and honey; beat at medium speed of an electric mixer until smooth. Stir in oats.

Pour about 1 cup batter onto preheated waffle iron coated with cooking spray. Bake 5 minutes or until done. Yield: 12 (4-inch square) waffles (136 calories each).

PROTEIN 5.5 / FAT 3.7 / CARBOHYDRATE 21.2 / FIBER 2.2 / CHOLESTEROL 46 / SODIUM 139 / POTASSIUM 165

GRAINS

Barley

BARLEY AND MUSHROOM BAKE

Vegetable cooking spray
2 teaspoons margarine
2 cups thinly sliced fresh mushrooms
1 cup chopped onion
1 cup barley, uncooked
2½ cups hot water
2 teaspoons beef-flavored bouillon granules
⅛ teaspoon pepper
2 tablespoons chopped fresh parsley

Coat a large skillet with cooking spray; add margarine. Place over medium heat until margarine melts. Add mushrooms and onion; sauté until tender. Add barley, and sauté 4 minutes or until barley is lightly browned. Remove from heat. Transfer to a 1½-quart baking dish coated with cooking spray.

Add the water, bouillon granules, and pepper to barley mixture. Cover and bake at 350° for 1 hour and 15 minutes, stirring at 15-minute intervals. Remove from oven, and gently stir in parsley. Yield: 8 servings (109 calories each).

PROTEIN 2.7 / FAT 1.5 / CARBOHYDRATE 22.2 / FIBER 1.9 / CHOLESTEROL 0 / SODIUM 129 / POTASSIUM 147

Bulgur

VEGETABLE BULGUR

---

1 (10¾-ounce) can chicken broth, undiluted
½ cup diced onion
½ cup diced leek
½ cup diced celery
1⅓ cups water
1 cup bulgur wheat, uncooked
⅛ teaspoon pepper

Combine first 4 ingredients in a 2-quart saucepan; cover and cook over medium heat 6 minutes. Add the water, and bring to a boil. Add bulgur. Cover; reduce heat, and simmer 20 minutes. Uncover and simmer 3 to 5 minutes or until liquid is absorbed. Season with pepper, and spoon into serving bowl. Yield: 6 (½-cup) servings (120 calories each).

PROTEIN 4.6 / FAT 0.8 / CARBOHYDRATE 24.2 / FIBER 0.8 / CHOLESTEROL 0 / SODIUM 173 / POTASSIUM 174

Couscous

VEGETABLE COUSCOUS

Vegetable cooking spray
2 medium-size yellow squash, diced
1 medium zucchini, diced
8 small fresh mushrooms, sliced
1 small sweet red pepper, seeded and diced
¼ cup plus 1 tablespoon reduced-calorie Italian salad
  dressing, divided
¼ cup water
¼ teaspoon salt
½ cup couscous, uncooked

Coat a large skillet with cooking spray, and place over medium heat until hot. Add yellow squash, zucchini, mushrooms, and red pepper; sauté until crisp-tender. Combine squash mixture and 3 tablespoons salad dressing in a large serving bowl; toss well. Set aside, and keep warm.

Combine the water, remaining 2 tablespoons salad dressing, and salt in a small saucepan; bring to a boil. Remove from heat, and stir in couscous. Continue to stir until all liquid is absorbed (about 3 minutes). Add to reserved vegetable mixture, and stir well. Yield: 8 servings (30 calories per serving).

PROTEIN 1.3 / FAT 0.2 / CARBOHYDRATE 6.3 / CHOLESTEROL 0 / IRON 0.5 / SODIUM 160 / CALCIUM 11

COUSCOUS WITH SUMMER VEGETABLES

Vegetable cooking spray
1 teaspoon olive oil
1¼ cups shredded zucchini
1¼ cups shredded carrot
½ cup chopped onion
1 small sweet red pepper, seeded and cut into ¼-inch strips
¼ cup chopped fresh parsley
1 tablespoon lemon juice
¼ teaspoon dried whole savory
¼ teaspoon dried whole rosemary, crumbled
¼ cup plus 2 tablespoons water
¼ teaspoon salt
½ cup couscous, uncooked

Coat a large nonstick skillet with cooking spray; add olive oil, and place over medium heat until hot. Add zucchini, carrot, onion, and red pepper; sauté until crisp-tender. Transfer to a large bowl; stir in parsley, lemon juice, savory, and rosemary. Set aside, and keep warm.

Combine the water and salt in a small saucepan, and bring to a boil. Remove from heat. Add couscous; cover and let stand 5 minutes or until couscous is tender and liquid is absorbed. Add to vegetable mixture, and stir well. Yield: 8 (½-cup) servings (35 calories each).

PROTEIN 1.1 / FAT 0.8 / CARBOHYDRATE 6.5 / CHOLESTEROL 0 / IRON 0.5 / SODIUM 81 / CALCIUM 16

Grits

BAKED CHEESE GRITS

2 cups water
¼ teaspoon salt
½ cup quick-cooking grits, uncooked
½ cup (2 ounces) shredded extra-sharp Cheddar cheese
1 egg, beaten
¼ cup skim milk
¼ teaspoon freshly ground black pepper
⅛ teaspoon Worcestershire sauce
Vegetable cooking spray

Bring the water and salt to a boil in a saucepan. Stir in grits; cover and reduce heat to low. Cook 5 minutes or until done, stirring occasionally.

Combine grits with next 5 ingredients, mixing well; pour into a 1-quart baking dish coated with cooking spray. Bake at 350° for 40 to 50 minutes or until lightly browned. Yield: 6 (½-cup) servings (100 calories).

PROTEIN 4.8 / FAT 4.2 / CARBOHYDRATE 10.8 / FIBER 0.1 / CHOLESTEROL 56 / SODIUM 174 / POTASSIUM 52

GRITS FLORENTINE

1 (10-ounce) package frozen chopped spinach
½ cup sliced green onions
¼ teaspoon ground white pepper
¼ teaspoon ground nutmeg
2½ cups water
¼ teaspoon salt
¾ cup quick-cooking grits, uncooked
½ cup plain nonfat yogurt

Cook chopped spinach according to package directions, omitting salt and adding green onions. Drain well; stir in white pepper and nutmeg. Set aside.

Combine the water and salt in a medium saucepan; bring to a boil. Stir in grits. Cover, reduce heat, and simmer 5 minutes or until thickened. Stir in reserved spinach mixture and yogurt. Continue cooking until thoroughly heated. Yield: 8 (½-cup) servings (69 calories each).

PROTEIN 3.2 / FAT 0.3 / CARBOHYDRATE 14.1 / CHOLESTEROL 0 / IRON 1.3 / SODIUM 111 / CALCIUM 72

Oats

BREAKFAST OATMEAL SPECIAL

1 cup skim milk
1 cup unsweetened apple juice
1 cup quick-cooking oats, uncooked
1 medium cooking apple, chopped
¼ cup dates, chopped
2 teaspoons honey
¼ teaspoon ground cinnamon
¼ teaspoon grated orange rind
Dash of ground cloves
3 tablespoons wheat germ

Combine skim milk and apple juice in a 1½-quart saucepan; bring to a boil. Add oats, apple, and dates; cook, stirring frequently, 1 minute. Remove from heat, and stir in honey, cinnamon, orange rind, and cloves. Cover and let stand 3 minutes.

Stir oatmeal; spoon into individual serving bowls. Sprinkle each serving with 1½ teaspoons wheat germ. Yield: 6 servings (134 calories each).

PROTEIN 4.6 / FAT 1.7 / CARBOHYDRATE 28.1 / FIBER 3.2 / CHOLESTEROL 1 / SODIUM 23 / POTASSIUM 265

Rice

HAWAIIAN RICE RING

1 cup short-grain rice, uncooked
¼ teaspoon salt
2¼ cups water, divided
¾ cup frozen English peas
Vegetable cooking spray
2 teaspoons unsalted margarine
½ cup chopped onion
½ cup chopped sweet red pepper
3 ounces turkey ham, diced
1 (8-ounce) can unsweetened crushed pineapple, drained
1 tablespoon low-sodium soy sauce
½ teaspoon ground ginger
Spinach leaves
Sweet red pepper strips (optional)
Green onion tops (optional)

Combine rice, salt, and 2 cups of the water in a heavy saucepan; bring to a boil. Cover, reduce heat, and simmer 15 to 20 minutes or until rice is tender and liquid is absorbed. Set aside.

Bring remaining ¼ cup water to a boil in a saucepan. Add peas. Cover, reduce heat, and simmer 5 minutes or until tender. Drain; set aside.

Coat a small nonstick skillet with cooking spray. Add margarine; place over medium-high heat until hot. Add chopped onion and red pepper, and sauté until tender. Combine reserved rice, peas, sautéed vegetables, ham, pineapple, soy sauce, and ginger, stirring until blended. Pack hot rice mixture into a 5-cup ring mold that has been coated with cooking spray. Invert onto a spinach leaf-lined serving plate. If desired, garnish with red pepper strips tied with green onion tops. Yield: 8 (½-cup) servings (141 calories each).

PROTEIN 4.8 / FAT 1.9 / CARBOHYDRATE 25.8 / CHOLESTEROL 6 / IRON 1.5 / SODIUM 239 / CALCIUM 16

WILD SPANISH RICE

1 (14½-ounce) can no-salt-added whole tomatoes,
   undrained
Vegetable cooking spray
¼ cup chopped onion
3 tablespoons chopped green pepper
1 stalk celery, chopped
⅔ cup wild rice, uncooked
1 teaspoon beef-flavored bouillon granules
¼ teaspoon prepared mustard

Drain tomatoes, reserving liquid. Coarsely chop tomatoes. Add enough water to reserved liquid to measure 1¼ cups. Set aside.

Coat a large nonstick skillet with cooking spray; place over medium-high heat until hot. Add onion, green pepper, and celery, and sauté until tender. Wash wild rice in 3 changes of hot water; drain. Add rice, reserved tomatoes and liquid, bouillon, and mustard to sautéed vegetable mixture; bring to a boil. Cover, reduce heat, and simmer 1 hour or until rice is tender and liquid is absorbed. Yield: 6 (½-cup) servings (84 calories each).

PROTEIN 3.2 / FAT 0.4 / CARBOHYDRATE 17.6 / CHOLESTEROL 0 / IRON 1.1 / SODIUM 179 / CALCIUM 32

SOUTH-OF-THE-BORDER RICE DRESSING

⅔ cup long-grain rice, uncooked
1⅓ cups water
1 cup cornmeal
½ teaspoon salt
½ teaspoon baking soda
1 cup skim milk
1 (8¾-ounce) can no-salt-added cream-style corn
2 eggs, beaten
½ cup chopped onion
2 tablespoons minced jalapeño pepper
1 tablespoon vegetable oil
Vegetable cooking spray
¾ cup (3 ounces) shredded Monterey Jack cheese with
  jalapeño peppers

Combine rice and the water in a medium saucepan; bring to a boil. Cover, reduce heat, and simmer 20 minutes or until rice is tender and liquid is absorbed. Set aside.

Combine cornmeal, salt, and baking soda in a large bowl; stir well. Add rice, skim milk, and next 5 ingredients, stirring well. Pour mixture into a 12- x 8- x 2-inch baking dish that has been coated with cooking spray. Bake, uncovered, at 350° for 45 minutes or until lightly browned. Sprinkle evenly with cheese, and bake an additional 5 minutes or until cheese melts. Yield: 12 (½-cup) servings (150 calories each).

PROTEIN 5.5 / FAT 4.6 / CARBOHYDRATE 21.7 / CHOLESTEROL 52 / IRON 1.0 / SODIUM 193 / CALCIUM 96

Whole Wheat Madeleines (page 27) keep the traditional madeleine shape, but with new, whole wheat goodness.

Made with a touch of red wine, honey, and mozzarella cheese, Eggplant Bread (page 21) tastes just as good as it looks.

Cranberry Orange Bread (page 25), Vermicelli with Tomato-Basil Sauce (page 78), Potato Crescents (page 11), Pear-Almond Muffins (page 30), Apple Danish (page 12), and Brown Rice Pilaf (page 58).

Spinach Noodles with Sautéed Vegetables (page 69).

Colorful Crab-Broccoli Macaroni (page 67) is made with surimi—an economical imitation crabmeat.

A spectacular selection of hearty, homemade breads that taste as good as they look! Clockwise from top left. Glazed Orange-Rum Buns (page 5), Poppy Seed-Onion Twists (page 36), Blueberry English Muffins (page 29), Cheddar Cheese Crescent Rolls (page 40), and Cracked Wheat-Zucchini Bread (page 15).

Sweet red pepper, yellow squash, and zucchini add bright color appeal to Vegetable Couscous (page 45).

Garlic and two types of cheese add flavor and creaminess to Straw and Hay (page 62).

Surprise your family with one of these homemade breads: (clockwise from top) Cranberry-Oatmeal Muffins (page 31), Granola Loaf (page 18), and Cardamom Coffee Braid (page 8).

Hawaiian Rice Ring (page 50) will be a flavorful complement to all types of entrées.

Couscous with Summer Vegetables (page 46) will complement all types of entrées, from mildly seasoned to spicy.

(Clockwise from top): Enjoy the home-baked goodness of Whole Wheat-Apricot Twist (page 26), Orange Rye Rolls (page 39), and Easy Cucumber-Dill Loaf (page 17).

APRICOT-RICE BAKE

Vegetable cooking spray
2 teaspoons margarine
1 cup long-grain rice, uncooked
½ cup chopped onion
¼ cup diced, dried apricots
¼ cup diced, dried, pitted prunes
2 cups water
2 teaspoons chicken-flavored bouillon granules
¼ teaspoon ground thyme
2 tablespoons sliced blanched almonds, toasted

Coat a large nonstick skillet with cooking spray; add margarine. Place over medium-high heat until hot; add rice and onion. Sauté until rice is browned and onion is tender.

Spoon rice mixture into a 1½-quart casserole that has been coated with cooking spray. Add apricots and prunes, stirring well. Combine the water, bouillon, and thyme in a large nonstick skillet; bring mixture to a boil. Pour over rice mixture. Cover and bake at 350° for 20 minutes or until rice is tender and liquid is absorbed. Sprinkle with almonds. Yield: 8 (½-cup) servings (127 calories each).

PROTEIN 2.3 / FAT 2.4 / CARBOHYDRATE 24.5 / CHOLESTEROL 0 / IRON 1.1 / SODIUM 219 / CALCIUM 17

WALDORF RICE

Vegetable cooking spray
¾ cup white rice, uncooked
1½ cups unsweetened apple juice
½ cup chopped celery
1 cup chopped baking apple
1 tablespoon lemon juice
¼ cup chopped pecans, toasted
Celery leaves (optional)

Coat a large skillet with cooking spray, and place over medium heat until hot. Add rice and cook, stirring frequently, until rice is lightly browned. Remove from heat, and slowly stir apple juice into rice.

Bring mixture to a boil. Cover; reduce heat to medium low, and cook 15 minutes. Stir in celery; cover and cook an additional 5 minutes or until liquid is absorbed and rice is tender.

Toss apple with lemon juice, and add to rice mixture. Stir in pecans. Transfer to a serving bowl, and garnish with celery leaves, if desired. Serve immediately. Yield: 8 servings (118 calories).

PROTEIN 1.5 / FAT 2.7 / CARBOHYDRATE 22.3 / CHOLESTEROL 0 / IRON 0.8 / SODIUM 9 / CALCIUM 13

WILD RICE WITH ARTICHOKES

¼ cup wild rice, uncooked
Vegetable cooking spray
½ cup parboiled rice, uncooked
1¼ cups water
1½ teaspoons chicken-flavored bouillon granules
¾ cup Chablis or other dry white wine
1 (9-ounce) package frozen artichoke hearts, thawed and chopped
4 ounces fresh mushrooms, sliced
1 small onion, chopped
1 clove garlic, minced
1 teaspoon fines herbes

Wash wild rice in a strainer under cold running water; drain.

Coat a large skillet with cooking spray; place over medium heat until hot. Add rice and cook, stirring frequently, until rice is lightly browned. Stir in remaining ingredients, and remove mixture from heat.

Place rice mixture in a 1½-quart baking dish; cover and bake at 350° for 1 hour or until all liquid is absorbed. Yield: 6 servings (110 calories each).

PROTEIN 3.8 / FAT 0.5 / CARBOHYDRATE 24.0 / CHOLESTEROL 0 / IRON 1.4 / SODIUM 120 / CALCIUM 31

PECAN–BROWN RICE PILAF

Vegetable cooking spray
½ cup chopped green onion
2½ cups water
1½ teaspoons chicken-flavored bouillon granules
½ teaspoon dried whole thyme
⅛ teaspoon pepper
1 cup brown rice, uncooked
¼ cup coarsely chopped pecans, toasted
2 tablespoons chopped fresh parsley
Fresh parsley sprigs (optional)

Coat a large saucepan with cooking spray; place over medium heat until hot. Add onion, and sauté until tender. Stir in next 4 ingredients; cover and bring to a boil. Add rice, and remove from heat.

Place rice mixture in a 1½-quart baking dish coated with cooking spray; cover and bake at 350° for 50 minutes or until liquid is absorbed. Stir in pecans and chopped parsley; garnish with parsley sprigs, if desired. Yield: 8 servings (112 calories each).

PROTEIN 2.2 / FAT 3.1 / CARBOHYDRATE 19.3 / FIBER 2.0 / CHOLESTEROL 0 / SODIUM 74 / POTASSIUM 86

ITALIAN RICE

Vegetable cooking spray
½ cup chopped onion
½ cup chopped green pepper
1 clove garlic, minced
2¼ cups water
¼ cup Chablis or other dry white wine
1½ teaspoons chicken-flavored bouillon granules
¾ teaspoon dried whole oregano
¾ teaspoon dried whole basil
⅛ teaspoon pepper
1 cup parboiled rice, uncooked
2 tablespoons chopped fresh parsley
2 tablespoons grated Parmesan cheese

Coat a large saucepan with cooking spray; place over medium heat until hot. Add onion, green pepper, and garlic; sauté until tender. Stir in next 6 ingredients. Cover; bring to a boil. Stir in rice. Cover; reduce heat, and simmer 20 minutes or until rice is tender and liquid is absorbed. Remove from heat; stir in parsley and cheese. Yield: 8 servings (98 calories each).

PROTEIN 2.4 / FAT 0.7 / CARBOHYDRATE 20.9 / FIBER 0.3 / CHOLESTEROL 1 / SODIUM 98 / POTASSIUM 95

BROWN RICE PILAF

¾ cup diced onion
1 (10¾-ounce) can chicken broth, undiluted and divided
1⅓ cups water
1 cup brown rice, uncooked
¾ cup finely chopped sweet red pepper
¾ cup finely chopped green pepper
¼ teaspoon dried whole thyme

Combine onion and ¼ cup chicken broth in a 2-quart ceramic ovenproof dish; cover and cook over medium heat 3 minutes or until onion is translucent, stirring frequently. Stir in remaining ingredients, and bring to a boil. Remove from heat. Cover and bake at 350° for 50 minutes or until liquid is absorbed. Yield: 8 (½-cup) servings (102 calories each).

PROTEIN 2.9 / FAT 0.8 / CARBOHYDRATE 20.7 / FIBER 2.1 / CHOLESTEROL 0 / SODIUM 124 / POTASSIUM 162

FRUITED WILD RICE

1 cup wild rice, uncooked
4 cups water
½ teaspoon salt
¼ pound pearl onions, peeled
1 (10¾-ounce) can chicken broth, undiluted
¼ cup currants
¼ cup golden raisins

Wash rice in cold water several times, and drain well. Bring 4 cups water and salt to a boil in a medium saucepan; add rice. Cover; reduce heat, and simmer 1 hour. Drain and set aside.

Combine onions and broth in a medium saucepan; bring to a boil. Cover; reduce heat, and simmer 25 minutes or until tender. Add currants, raisins, and reserved rice; cover and cook over low heat

2 to 3 minutes or until thoroughly heated, stirring occasionally. Spoon into a serving bowl to serve. Yield: 7 (½-cup) servings (125 calories each).

PROTEIN 4.7 / FAT 0.6 / CARBOHYDRATE 26.8 / FIBER 0.5 / CHOLESTEROL 0 / SODIUM 310 / POTASSIUM 209

MUSHROOM RISOTTO

2 cups sliced fresh mushrooms
2 tablespoons minced shallot
1 tablespoon lemon juice
Vegetable cooking spray
1 cup Italian Arborio rice
2 cups hot water
1 teaspoon chicken-flavored bouillon granules
2 tablespoons grated Parmesan cheese
¼ teaspoon pepper

Combine mushrooms, shallot, and lemon juice in a nonstick saucepan coated with cooking spray. Cover and cook over medium heat 5 minutes or until tender, stirring occasionally. Stir in rice, and cook 3 minutes, stirring occasionally.

Combine the hot water and bouillon; add ½ cup bouillon mixture to rice mixture. Cook 2 to 3 minutes or until liquid is absorbed, stirring occasionally. Repeat procedure with remaining bouillon mixture, adding ½ cup at a time and making sure each portion is absorbed before adding the next.

Remove from heat; stir in cheese and pepper. Spoon into a serving bowl to serve. Yield: 6 (½-cup) servings (138 calories each).

PROTEIN 3.6 / FAT 0.8 / CARBOHYDRATE 28.8 / FIBER 1.0 / CHOLESTEROL 1 / SODIUM 98 / POTASSIUM 136

PASTAS

Cannelloni

TURKEY CANNELLONI

---

1 (8-ounce) package cannelloni shells, uncooked
1 (10-ounce) package frozen chopped spinach, thawed
4 cups no-salt-added tomato juice
1 (6-ounce) can no-salt-added tomato paste
1½ teaspoons dried whole chervil
1 teaspoon dried whole basil
¼ teaspoon garlic powder
Vegetable cooking spray
½ (1-pound) package raw ground turkey, thawed
¾ cup chopped fresh mushrooms
½ cup chopped onion
1 clove garlic, crushed
⅛ teaspoon pepper
1 (8-ounce) package Neufchâtel cheese, softened
2 eggs
1 cup (4 ounces) shredded part-skim mozzarella cheese, divided

Cook cannelloni shells according to package directions, omitting salt. Drain, and set aside. Drain thawed spinach; squeeze out excess moisture between paper towels, and set aside.

Combine tomato juice and next 4 ingredients, stirring well. Spread 2 cups tomato mixture in a 13- x 9- x 2-inch baking dish coated with cooking spray. Set aside remaining tomato mixture.

Combine turkey, mushrooms, onion, garlic, and pepper in a

large skillet. Cook over medium heat until turkey is browned, stirring to crumble. Drain in a colander; pat with a paper towel to remove excess grease. Set aside.

Beat Neufchâtel cheese and eggs until smooth. Stir in spinach, turkey mixture, and ½ cup mozzarella cheese. Stuff cannelloni shells, and place in baking dish. Top with remaining tomato mixture. Cover and bake at 350° for 30 to 40 minutes. Uncover; sprinkle with remaining ½ cup mozzarella cheese. Let stand, covered, 10 minutes. Serve immediately. Yield: 8 servings (338 calories each).

PROTEIN 23.0 / FAT 12.2 / CARBOHYDRATE 35.4 / CHOLESTEROL 120 / IRON 2.9 / SODIUM 266 / CALCIUM 187

Cappellini

CAPPELLINI WITH BROCCOLI AND CHEESE

6 ounces cappellini, uncooked
1 pound fresh broccoli
Vegetable cooking spray
2 teaspoons olive oil
1 cup canned low-sodium chicken broth, undiluted
2 cups peeled, seeded, and chopped tomatoes
½ cup (2 ounces) goat cheese
2 tablespoons sesame seeds, toasted
¼ teaspoon freshly ground pepper

Prepare cappellini according to package directions, omitting salt and fat. Drain; set aside.

Wash and trim fresh broccoli; cut into small flowerets, and cut stems diagonally into 1-inch pieces.

Coat a large nonstick skillet with cooking spray; add olive oil.

Place over medium heat until hot. Add broccoli, and sauté 3 minutes or until crisp-tender. Add chicken broth, and bring to a boil; stir in tomatoes and goat cheese. Reduce heat, and stir until cheese melts. Stir in reserved cappellini. Add sesame seeds and pepper; toss gently. Serve immediately. Yield: 16 (½-cup) servings (69 calories each).

PROTEIN 2.6 / FAT 2.1 / CARBOHYDRATE 9.9 / CHOLESTEROL 3 / IRON 0.7 / SODIUM 44 / CALCIUM 40

Fettuccine

STRAW AND HAY

1 cup skim milk
½ cup low-fat cottage cheese
1 tablespoon cornstarch
½ cup freshly grated Parmesan cheese, divided
¼ teaspoon salt
⅛ teaspoon freshly ground pepper
⅛ teaspoon ground nutmeg
Vegetable cooking spray
4 ounces diced lean cooked ham
1 clove garlic, crushed
½ cup frozen English peas
4 ounces fettuccine, uncooked
4 ounces spinach fettuccine, uncooked

Combine skim milk, cottage cheese, and cornstarch in container of a food processor or electric blender; process until smooth. Transfer milk mixture to a medium nonstick skillet. Place over medium heat; add ¼ cup Parmesan cheese, salt, pepper, and nutmeg, stirring until cheese melts. Set aside.

Coat a large nonstick skillet with cooking spray; place over medium heat until hot. Add ham and garlic; sauté 2 minutes. Stir in peas, and sauté 2 minutes. Remove from heat, and stir in reserved milk mixture. Set aside.

Cook fettuccine and spinach fettuccine according to package directions, omitting salt and fat; drain. Place in a large bowl; pour ham mixture over pasta, tossing gently until well combined. Sprinkle with remaining ¼ cup Parmesan cheese. Serve immediately. Yield: 12 (½-cup) servings (118 calories each).

PROTEIN 8.6 / FAT 3.0 / CARBOHYDRATE 14.6 / CHOLESTEROL 30 / IRON 1.1 / SODIUM 325 / CALCIUM 108

Linguine

LINGUINE WITH RED CLAM SAUCE

Vegetable cooking spray
1 cup chopped onion
1 clove garlic, minced
1 (6-ounce) can tomato paste
1 cup diced tomato
1 teaspoon dried whole basil
1 teaspoon dried whole oregano
⅛ teaspoon pepper
1 bay leaf
½ cup dry red wine
2 (6½-ounce) cans minced clams, rinsed and drained
½ (16-ounce) package linguine, uncooked

Coat a medium skillet with cooking spray, and place over low heat until hot. Add onion and garlic; sauté 5 minutes. Add next 7 ingredients. Bring to a boil. Cover; reduce heat, and simmer 30 minutes. Add clams; cover and simmer 30 minutes. Discard bay leaf.

Cook linguine according to package directions, omitting salt and fat; drain.

Combine red clam sauce and linguine in a large bowl, tossing gently. Serve immediately. Yield: 4 main-dish servings (311 calories each).

PROTEIN 15.4 / FAT 2.2 / CARBOHYDRATE 58.4 / FIBER 2.7 / CHOLESTEROL 22 / SODIUM 78 / POTASSIUM 760

MEDITERRANEAN LINGUINE

6 ounces whole wheat linguine, uncooked
Vegetable cooking spray
1 cup sliced fresh mushrooms
1 medium-size green pepper, seeded and cut into thin strips
1 medium-size sweet red pepper, seeded and cut into thin strips
1 clove garlic, minced
1 (14-ounce) can artichoke hearts, drained and quartered
½ cup reduced-calorie Italian salad dressing
3 tablespoons sliced, pitted ripe olives
1 tablespoon chopped fresh parsley
½ cup (2 ounces) shredded mozzarella cheese

Cook linguine according to package directions, omitting salt; drain. Transfer to a large bowl, and keep warm.

Coat a large skillet with cooking spray; place over medium heat until hot. Add mushrooms, green pepper, red pepper, and garlic; sauté until crisp-tender. Add artichokes, salad dressing, olives, and parsley; stir well, and heat thoroughly. Add to reserved linguine; toss gently. Sprinkle with mozzarella cheese, and serve immediately. Yield: 12 servings (91 calories each).

PROTEIN 3.7 / FAT 1.9 / CARBOHYDRATE 15.6 / FIBER 1.8 / CHOLESTEROL 4 / SODIUM 139 / POTASSIUM 186

Macaroni

JALEPEÑO MACARONI AND CHEESE

1 (8-ounce) package elbow macaroni, uncooked
1 cup evaporated skim milk
1 tablespoon cornstarch
¾ cup (3 ounces) shredded Monterey Jack cheese with jalapeño peppers
2 green onions, finely chopped
2 tablespoons diced green pepper
¼ teaspoon salt
1 (2-ounce) jar diced pimiento, drained
1 tablespoon chopped fresh parsley

Cook macaroni according to package directions, omitting salt and fat. Drain and set aside.

Combine evaporated skim milk and cornstarch in a medium saucepan; stir with a wire whisk until smooth. Cook over medium heat until thickened, stirring frequently. Stir in cheese and next 4 ingredients.

Combine macaroni and cheese mixture, stirring well. Transfer mixture to a serving dish; sprinkle with parsley. Serve immediately. Yield: 8 (½-cup) servings (176 calories each).

PROTEIN 8.7 / FAT 3.7 / CARBOHYDRATE 26.5 / CHOLESTEROL 10 / IRON 1.2 / SODIUM 169 / CALCIUM 183

VEGETABLE GARDEN-PASTA MEDLEY

1 small zucchini, cut into julienne strips
1 pint cherry tomatoes, halved
¼ cup sliced, pitted ripe olives
2 cloves garlic, minced
½ teaspoon dried whole oregano
½ teaspoon dried whole basil
¼ cup chopped fresh parsley
¼ teaspoon salt
⅛ teaspoon coarsely ground pepper
½ cup plain low-fat yogurt
1 tablespoon plus 1½ teaspoons olive oil
6 ounces corkscrew pasta, uncooked

Combine all ingredients except pasta in a large bowl, tossing well. Cover and let stand at room temperature 1 hour.

Cook pasta according to package directions, omitting salt and fat; drain. Combine pasta and vegetable mixture in a large saucepan. Cook over medium heat 5 minutes or until thoroughly heated. Serve immediately. Yield: 12 (1-cup) servings (86 calories each).

PROTEIN 2.8 / FAT 2.4 / CARBOHYDRATE 13.7 / CHOLESTEROL 1 / IRON 0.8 / SODIUM 80 / CALCIUM 32

COLORFUL CRAB-BROCCOLI MACARONI

1 (8-ounce) package medium shell macaroni, uncooked
Vegetable cooking spray
⅓ cup chopped green onions
3 cloves garlic, minced
2 teaspoons unsalted margarine
1 tablespoon all-purpose flour
½ cup Chablis or other dry white wine
¼ cup skim milk
¾ teaspoon dried whole basil
½ teaspoon dried whole dillweed
1 small sweet yellow pepper, seeded and cut into ½-inch
   pieces
½ pound fresh broccoli, coarsely chopped
½ (1-pound) package frozen imitation crabmeat, thawed,
   rinsed, and drained
Fresh basil sprigs (optional)

Cook macaroni according to package directions, omitting salt and fat. Drain; set aside.

Coat a large nonstick skillet with cooking spray; place over medium-high heat until hot. Add green onions and garlic, and sauté until crisp-tender. Remove from skillet, and set aside.

Melt margarine in skillet. Add flour; cook over medium heat, stirring constantly, 1 minute. Gradually stir in wine; cook over medium heat, stirring constantly, until mixture is thickened and bubbly. Remove from heat, gradually stir in skim milk, basil, and dillweed.

Add onion mixture, yellow pepper, broccoli, and crabmeat to sauce. Simmer 5 minutes or until vegetables are crisp-tender. Combine pasta and broccoli mixture; toss gently. Garnish with fresh basil sprigs, if desired. Yield: 6 (1-cup) servings (218 calories each).

PROTEIN 11.1 / FAT 2.4 / CARBOHYDRATE 38.3 / CHOLESTEROL 0 / IRON 2.2 / SODIUM 335 / CALCIUM 163

Noodles

WINE–BRAISED BELL PEPPERS AND ONIONS WITH BROAD NOODLES

1 large sweet red pepper
1 large sweet yellow pepper
Vegetable cooking spray
1½ teaspoons olive oil
1 medium-size yellow onion, cut into ¾-inch-thick slices
¼ cup Chablis or other dry white wine
4 ounces pappardelle, uncooked
1 tablespoon minced fresh parsley
1 tablespoon chopped fresh basil
1 teaspoon balsamic vinegar
¼ teaspoon salt
¼ teaspoon freshly ground pepper

Wash and dry peppers. Place peppers on a baking sheet. Broil 4 inches from heat 2 to 3 minutes on each side or until skins are blackened and charred. Immediately transfer peppers to a large brown paper bag. Roll top tightly to trap steam; let peppers steam 20 minutes. Unroll top, and allow steam to escape; carefully remove peppers. Remove and discard skins and seeds. Cut peppers into ¾-inch strips; set aside.

Coat a large nonstick skillet with cooking spray; add olive oil. Place over medium-high heat until hot. Add onion, and sauté until tender. Add reserved pepper strips and wine. Bring to a boil; reduce heat, and simmer 1 minute. Cover and simmer an additional 5 minutes.

Cook pasta according to package directions, omitting salt and fat; drain. Combine pasta, pepper mixture, and remaining ingredients, tossing gently. Yield: 8 (½-cup) servings (81 calories each).

PROTEIN 2.5 / FAT 1.8 / CARBOHYDRATE 14.1 / CHOLESTEROL 13 / IRON 1.2 / SODIUM 76 / CALCIUM 23

SPINACH NOODLES WITH SAUTÉED VEGETABLES

6 ounces spinach noodles, uncooked
Vegetable cooking spray
1 medium onion, coarsely chopped
1 clove garlic, crushed
1 medium-size yellow squash, thinly sliced
1 medium zucchini, thinly sliced
1 cup fresh corn, cut from cob
1 tablespoon chopped fresh parsley
¾ teaspoon dried whole basil
¾ teaspoon dried whole oregano
¼ teaspoon salt
¼ teaspoon freshly ground pepper
2 medium tomatoes, peeled and chopped

Cook spinach noodles according to package directions, omitting salt; drain. Transfer to a serving platter, and keep warm.

Coat a large skillet with cooking spray; place over medium heat until hot. Add onion and garlic; sauté 3 minutes or until tender. Add next 8 ingredients; sauté 4 minutes or until vegetables are tender. (Do not overcook.) Stir in tomatoes. Serve vegetables over warm spinach noodles. Yield: 10 servings (77 calories each).

PROTEIN 3.0 / FAT 1.5 / CARBOHYDRATE 14.1 / FIBER 1.1 / CHOLESTEROL 23 / SODIUM 74 / POTASSIUM 251

CALIENTE NOODLES

4 ounces medium egg noodles, uncooked
Vegetable cooking spray
1 teaspoon vegetable oil
1 small onion, chopped
1 (14½-ounce) can no-salt-added stewed tomatoes,
　undrained and chopped
2 jalapeño peppers, seeded and chopped
¼ cup (1 ounce) shredded sharp Cheddar cheese

Cook noodles according to package directions, omitting salt. Drain, and set aside.

Coat a skillet with cooking spray; add vegetable oil, and place over medium heat until hot. Add onion, and sauté until tender. Remove from heat. Combine onion, reserved noodles, and remaining ingredients except cheese in a medium bowl, stirring well. Spoon mixture into a 1½-quart casserole coated with cooking spray; sprinkle with cheese. Cover and bake at 350° for 25 to 30 minutes or until thoroughly heated. Yield: 4 servings (180 calories each).

PROTEIN 6.5 / FAT 4.8 / CARBOHYDRATE 28.3 / CHOLESTEROL 32 / IRON 1.5 / SODIUM 65 / CALCIUM 97

CHICKEN-NOODLE PARMESAN

1 (8-ounce) package medium egg noodles, uncooked
¼ cup chopped fresh parsley
Vegetable cooking spray
½ cup chopped onion
2 cloves garlic, minced
1 (28-ounce) can no-salt-added whole tomatoes,
　undrained
1 (8-ounce) can no-salt-added tomato sauce
¼ teaspoon ground oregano

¼ teaspoon pepper
⅓ cup fine, dry breadcrumbs
3 tablespoons grated Parmesan cheese
1 egg, beaten
1 tablespoon water
6 (4-ounce) skinned, boned chicken breast halves, cut
 into 1-inch pieces
1 tablespoon vegetable oil
½ cup (2 ounces) shredded part-skim mozzarella cheese

Cook noodles according to package directions, omitting salt and fat. Drain; stir in parsley, and set aside.

Coat a large nonstick skillet with cooking spray; place over medium-high heat until hot. Add onion and garlic, and sauté until tender. Set aside.

Drain tomatoes; reserve ½ cup liquid. Coarsely chop tomatoes. Add tomatoes, ½ cup tomato liquid, tomato sauce, oregano, and pepper to reserved onion mixture. Set aside.

Combine breadcrumbs and Parmesan cheese in a small bowl. Combine egg and water in a small bowl. Dip chicken into egg mixture; dredge in breadcrumb mixture.

Coat a large nonstick skillet with cooking spray; add vegetable oil. Place over medium-high heat until hot; add chicken, and cook 3 to 5 minutes or until lightly browned.

Coat a 13- x 9- x 2-inch baking dish with cooking spray. Spoon noodles into dish. Arrange chicken over noodles. Pour reserved tomato mixture over chicken. Sprinkle with mozzarella cheese. Bake, uncovered, at 350° for 25 minutes. Yield: 8 servings (300 calories each).

PROTEIN 26.9 / FAT 6.7 / CARBOHYDRATE 31.8 / CHOLESTEROL 104 / IRON 2.3 / SODIUM 179 / CALCIUM 137

Rigatoni

RIGATONI WITH CURRIED VEGETABLES

½ (16-ounce) package rigatoni or other tubular pasta, uncooked
1⅓ cups chopped green onion
1 medium carrot, scraped and coarsely grated
1 medium-size green pepper, seeded and cut into julienne strips
1 medium zucchini, coarsely grated
½ cup water
½ teaspoon chicken-flavored bouillon granules
2 cups cauliflower flowerets
1 cup broccoli flowerets
2 teaspoons curry powder
¾ cup plain low-fat yogurt
¼ cup sour cream
2 tablespoons minced fresh parsley or coriander
1 tablespoon lemon juice

Cook rigatoni according to package directions, omitting salt; drain well. Set aside, and keep warm.

Combine green onion, carrot, green pepper, zucchini, water, and bouillon granules in a Dutch oven; bring to a boil. Reduce heat, and cook, uncovered, 5 minutes, stirring occasionally. Add cauliflower and broccoli; simmer 5 minutes or until tender. Stir in curry powder; simmer 2 minutes. Stir in remaining ingredients, and cook over medium-low heat until thoroughly heated, stirring occasionally. (Do not boil.) Serve over warm pasta. Yield: 8 side-dish servings (160 calories each).

PROTEIN 6.4 / FAT 2.5 / CARBOHYDRATE 28.8 / FIBER 2.0 / CHOLESTEROL 4 / SODIUM 55 / POTASSIUM 383

DILLED RIGATONI

½ (8-ounce) package Neufchâtel cheese, softened
¼ cup hot water
2 teaspoons chopped green onion
1 teaspoon lemon juice
½ teaspoon dried whole dillweed
¼ teaspoon salt
½ (16-ounce) package rigatoni, uncooked

Beat Neufchâtel cheese in a medium bowl until fluffy. Gradually add the hot water, beating until smooth. Stir in green onion, lemon juice, dillweed, and salt; set aside.

Cook rigatoni according to package directions, omitting salt; drain well. Add rigatoni to reserved Neufchâtel mixture, tossing gently. Serve immediately. Yield: 8 servings (142 calories each).

PROTEIN 5.0 / FAT 3.7 / CARBOHYDRATE 21.9 / FIBER 0.7 / CHOLESTEROL 11 / SODIUM 131 / POTASSIUM 76

Shells

BLUE CHEESE PASTA SHELLS

4 ounces shell macaroni, uncooked
½ cup chopped green onions
5 radishes, thinly sliced
¼ cup crumbled blue cheese
1 tablespoon chopped fresh parsley
¼ cup reduced-calorie mayonnaise
1 tablespoon lemon juice
⅛ teaspoon pepper

Cook macaroni according to package directions, omitting salt; drain well.

Combine macaroni, green onions, radishes, blue cheese, and parsley in a medium mixing bowl; toss gently. Combine mayonnaise, lemon juice, and pepper in a 1-cup glass measure, mixing well; add to macaroni mixture. Toss gently and chill thoroughly. Yield: 4 servings (151 calories each).

PROTEIN 4.6 / FAT 6.4 / CARBOHYDRATE 18.9 / CHOLESTEROL 10 / IRON 0.9 / SODIUM 215 / CALCIUM 53

Spaghetti

SPAGHETTI WITH SPRING VEGETABLES

1 (16-ounce) package spaghetti, uncooked
¼ pound fresh green beans
Vegetable cooking spray
1 medium onion, thinly sliced
1 clove garlic, minced
1 medium carrot, scraped and coarsely grated
1 medium-size sweet red or green pepper, seeded and cut
    into julienne strips
½ cup water
½ teaspoon chicken-flavored bouillon granules
¼ pound fresh asparagus, cut into ¾-inch pieces
½ cup fresh English peas
½ cup plain low-fat yogurt
½ cup sour cream
2 tablespoons lemon juice
⅓ cup minced fresh parsley
1 tablespoon minced chives
¼ teaspoon dried whole tarragon or 1 tablespoon minced
    fresh tarragon
¼ teaspoon dried whole basil or 1 tablespoon minced
    fresh basil
⅛ teaspoon pepper

Cook spaghetti according to package directions, omitting salt; drain well. Set aside, and keep warm.

Remove strings from beans, and cut into ¾-inch pieces; set aside. Coat a large Dutch oven with cooking spray; place over medium heat until hot. Add onion and garlic, and sauté 5 minutes or until tender. Add carrot and red pepper; cook 2 minutes, stirring constantly. Add the water, bouillon, asparagus, peas, and reserved green beans; cook, covered, 8 minutes or until vegetables are crisp-tender. Add remaining ingredients; cook until thoroughly heated, stirring frequently. (Do not allow sauce to boil). Serve over warm pasta. Yield: 16 side-dish servings (140 calories each).

PROTEIN 5.0 / FAT 2.1 / CARBOHYDRATE 25.4 / FIBER 1.4 / CHOLESTEROL 4 / SODIUM 29 / POTASSIUM 179

Spaghettini

SPAGHETTINI WITH SUN-COOKED TOMATO SAUCE

3 cups peeled, seeded, and chopped tomatoes
12 Calamata olives, pitted and quartered
2 tablespoons capers
1 tablespoon olive oil
1 clove garlic, minced
¼ teaspoon salt
¼ teaspoon crushed red pepper
⅛ teaspoon freshly ground pepper
8 ounces spaghettini, uncooked
¼ cup shredded fresh basil

Combine first 8 ingredients in a large glass bowl; toss gently. Cover and put in a warm place outside in sun or in kitchen for 3 hours.

Cook pasta according to package directions, omitting salt and fat; drain well.

Add hot pasta and basil to sun-cooked tomato sauce; toss well. Yield: 8 (1-cup) servings (150 calories each).

PROTEIN 4.8 / FAT 3.0 / CARBOHYDRATE 26.9 / CHOLESTEROL 0 / IRON 2.2 / SODIUM 363 / CALCIUM 56

Vermicelli

BROCCOLI VERMICELLI

---

4 ounces vermicelli, uncooked
1 teaspoon vegetable oil
2 cups broccoli flowerets
⅓ cup chopped onion
½ cup (2 ounces) shredded Swiss cheese
2 tablespoons grated Parmesan cheese
¼ teaspoon salt
⅛ teaspoon garlic powder
⅛ teaspoon dried whole thyme
⅛ teaspoon ground nutmeg

Cook vermicelli according to package directions, omitting salt; drain. Toss with vegetable oil in a large bowl, and keep warm.

Cook broccoli and onion, covered, in a small amount of boiling water 5 minutes or until crisp-tender. Drain well.

Add broccoli, onion, cheeses, salt, garlic powder, thyme, and nutmeg to reserved vermicelli. Toss gently until cheese melts. Transfer to a serving bowl, and serve immediately. Yield: 6 servings (132 calories).

PROTEIN 6.7 / FAT 4.2 / CARBOHYDRATE 16.9 / FIBER 1.2 / CHOLESTEROL 10 / SODIUM 162 / POTASSIUM 161

VERMICELLI WITH TOMATO-BASIL SAUCE

½ (16-ounce) package vermicelli, uncooked
Vegetable cooking spray
2 cloves garlic, minced
1 medium onion, thinly sliced
5 medium tomatoes, peeled and chopped
1 (8-ounce) can unsalted tomato sauce
1 tablespoon dried whole basil or ¼ cup minced fresh
   basil
⅛ teaspoon pepper
2 tablespoons grated Parmesan cheese

Cook vermicelli according to package directions, omitting salt; drain and set aside.

Coat a Dutch oven with cooking spray; place over medium heat until hot. Add garlic and onion; sauté 5 minutes or until tender. Stir in tomato, tomato sauce, basil, and pepper; simmer 15 minutes. Stir in vermicelli, and cook over low heat until thoroughly heated, stirring occasionally. Transfer to a large platter, and sprinkle with Parmesan cheese to serve. Yield: 8 side-dish servings (143 calories each).

PROTEIN 5.4 / FAT 0.9 / CARBOHYDRATE 28.5 / FIBER 0.9 / CHOLESTEROL 1 / SODIUM 33 / POTASSIUM 264

EGGPLANT VERMICELLI

4 ounces vermicelli, uncooked
Vegetable cooking spray
1 teaspoon olive oil
1 cup peeled and cubed eggplant
1 cup finely chopped onion
2 cloves garlic, minced
1½ teaspoons dried whole basil
1½ teaspoons dried whole oregano
¼ teaspoon crushed red pepper
1 small zucchini, thinly sliced
¼ pound fresh mushrooms, sliced
2 large tomatoes, chopped
1 tablespoon plus 2 teaspoons grated Parmesan cheese

Cook vermicelli according to package directions, omitting salt. Drain, and set aside.

Coat a large skillet with cooking spray; add olive oil, and place over medium-high heat until hot. Add eggplant and next 5 ingredients. Sauté until vegetables are tender. Add zucchini, mushrooms, and tomatoes; sauté 2 minutes or until mixture is thoroughly heated. Combine reserved vermicelli and vegetable mixture on a large serving platter; toss gently. Sprinkle with Parmesan cheese. Yield: 6 servings (124 calories each).

PROTEIN 5.0 / FAT 1.8 / CARBOHYDRATE 23.4 / CHOLESTEROL 1 / IRON 1.7 / SODIUM 37 / CALCIUM 58

Ziti

ZITI SALAD WITH AVOCADO SAUCE

1 (16-ounce) package ziti, uncooked
¾ cup plain low-fat yogurt
1 medium-size green chile pepper, seeded and minced
¼ cup minced fresh parsley or coriander
3 tablespoons lemon juice
1 clove garlic, minced
¼ teaspoon salt
⅛ teaspoon pepper
1 medium avocado, cubed and divided
1 medium-size sweet red or green pepper, seeded and chopped
2 medium tomatoes, seeded and chopped
½ cup minced green onion

Cook ziti according to package directions, omitting salt; drain and set aside.

Combine yogurt, chile pepper, parsley, lemon juice, garlic, salt, pepper, and ½ cup avocado in container of an electric blender; process until pureed. Combine avocado sauce and ziti in a large bowl; add remaining avocado, red pepper, tomato, and green onion; toss gently. Cover and chill 1 to 2 hours. Yield: 8 main-dish servings (278 calories each).

PROTEIN 9.3 / FAT 5.0 / CARBOHYDRATE 49.6 / FIBER 2.8 / CHOLESTEROL 1 / SODIUM 97 / POTASSIUM 452

INDEX

Rye
  green onion bread, 22–23
  orange rolls, 39–40
  and raisin buns, 4–5

Salad
  ziti with avocado sauce, 80
Sauce
  avocado, 80
  tomato, sun-cooked, 76
  tomato-basil, 78
Sausage and pepper braid, 19–20
Seafood
  crab-broccoli macaroni, 67
Shells
  blue cheese pasta, 74
Spaghetti with spring vegetables, 75–76
Spaghettini with sun-cooked tomato sauce,
  76
Spanish rice, wild, 51
Spices
  cardamom coffee braid, 8
  curried vegetables with rigatoni, 72
  gingered applesauce waffles, 41–42
  poppy seed–onion twists, 36–37
Spinach
  grits Florentine, 48
  noodles with sautéed vegetables, 69
Straw and hay, 62–63
Sweet potato bread, 24–25
Swiss cheese–mushroom rolls, 37–38

Tomato
  -mozzarella bread, 16
  -basil sauce, 78
  suncooked, 76

Turkey cannelloni, 60–61

Vegetable(s)
  bulgur, 44
  couscous, 45
  couscous with summer vegetables, 46
  curried, with rigatoni, 72
  garden-pasta medley, 66
  sautéed, with spinach noodles, 69
  spaghetti with spring vegetables, 75–76
  See also specific name
Vermicelli
  broccoli, 77
  eggplant, 79
  with tomato-basil sauce, 78

Waffles
  applesauce, gingered, 41–42
  oatmeal–whole wheat, 42
Waldorf rice, 54
Whole wheat
  -apple pancakes, 34
  -apricot twist, 26
  madeleines, 27
  -oatmeal waffles, 42
  -onion bagels, 1–2
  popovers, 35
Wild rice
  with artichokes, 55
  fruited, 58–59
  Spanish, 51
Wine-braised bell peppers and onions with
    broad noodles, 68

Ziti salad with avocado sauce, 80
Zucchini–cracked wheat bread, 15–16